MW01091737

The HOUSE ROMANTIC

A portrait of designer
Georgia Tapert Howe,
by Enoc Perez, in
Georgia's dining room
in Los Angeles

The HOUSE ROMANTIC

Curating Memorable Interiors for a Meaningful Life

HASKELL HARRIS

Photographs by Charlotte Zacharkiw

Watercolor Illustrations by Lia Burke Libaire

ABRAMS, NEW YORK

*To my parents, the
original house romantics.
And to Wiley, my
constant companion in
creativity.*

CONTENTS

"As I entered I would leave nurturing of my home, but in would take their me. *The lessons the feelings of belonging* that into my character my companions

this world,
behind the
family and my
another sense I
protection with
I had learned,
groundedness and
have been woven
there, would be
on the journey."

—SIDNEY POITIER

FOREWORD

by Anna Spiro

I met Haskell back in my days of blogging and, as many people did back then, we found each other through a common love for homes, interiors, gardens, and style. She has such a kind and warm heart, which I was instantly drawn to, and when I read her story about her own journey of loving and leaving a home, I couldn't believe that we had shared such a similar path.

As I read the wonderful stories throughout this beautiful book that Haskell has compiled, I can't help but feel a true connection with the sentiment and feelings that have been shared. All the houses and rooms have been carefully put together. There is no blandness, only interesting things with not one space looking like another. This book is a celebration of individual style and people who understand the life-changing experience of creating a home that has comfort, meaning, flair, authenticity, nature, and soul.

The very first house I remember living in was an old timber house with a beautiful, overflowing garden. I was six at the time. I have wonderful memories of running wild and free in that beautiful place, picking flowers, and setting up roadside flower stalls. The next house we lived in was a modern house with a pool and a tree house. I will never forget the Yves Klein Blue carpet mum had in the sitting room that she pared with crisp white sofas and plain lemon silk cushions. I spent a lot of time as a young girl rearranging my bedroom and drawing on my bedroom walls, much to mum's disapproval.

My creativity sprouted within the gardens and beautiful rooms mum decorated with her fabulous style—she taught me how to be an aesthete. This unintentional education and way of living that my parents exposed me to has shaped me, and now, I am doing the very same thing with my sons. I have exposed them to a life that is full of creativity, and the homes we have lived in have shaped them and are part of their life journeys.

When I was in my late teens, I started working as a junior interior decorator for a well-established designer. I was living at home and redecorating my bedroom like I always did. I still own the very first piece

Anna's mix of textiles, prints, and antiques never fails to enchant.

This page:
Anna's colorful take
on bathing in style

Opposite:
Her kitchen in
Elsternwick,
Australia

of furniture I bought with my own money when I was seventeen. I remember trying to work out how I would pay for it. I ended up putting the lovely antique chest of drawers on layaway and I committed to a twelve-week payment plan with the seller. I have kept that piece of furniture with me since that time, and when I look at it, it reminds me of the journey I've had—the ups, the downs, and all the roundabouts. It's been there with me like a loyal friend and confidant, and now my boys love it too as they know how special it is to me. I'm sure when I'm long gone, it, along with a lot of my furniture and art, will be kept and cherished by them as a small piece of me that holds memories for them throughout their lives.

From an early age I started a tradition that I still keep today. When we would leave a house to move into a new house, I would say a goodbye speech to the house we were leaving, thanking it for having us and wishing it well with its new family. These quiet speeches would always end in me breaking down in tears. It's a really hard thing leaving a house, especially one you truly love, that has been a place of comfort, safety, joy, sadness, and happiness.

About four years ago, I left a house that I thought was going to be our forever house. It was a magnificent old property. However, our lives changed, and due to my husband and I deciding to go our separate ways, we made the difficult decision to sell our beautiful old family home. This was the home my children cherished even more than I did. It was a very hard time.

With a few passing years since leaving our old family home and a lot of reflection, I have come to realize that although the homes we live in are so very, very precious, it's the people, the furniture, the art, and collections that you fill a home with that really matter. These pieces move with us on our journey and hold the key to unlocking the stories of our past. When we move in and out of homes and places, whether it's by choice, or circumstance, it's the pieces you take with you that can make a new house feel just like home, as their familiarity is what makes us feel comforted and safe. As our lives pass us by, we can sit in a room of a new house and be surrounded by all our old friends and feel true comfort knowing that they have and always will be there to make us feel perfectly at home. ■

Opposite: Color in unexpected places, like this vibrant mantel, is textbook Anna.
All photos by Martina Gemmola

In the living room of the house on *Grove Street*, with my grandmother's wingback chair, reimagined in a playful fabric by Ottoline

INTRODUCTION

My colleagues, friends, and family might say I am *more* than passionate about houses. They are likely to use stronger words: a *dreamer*, a *romantic*, a person who idealizes the concept of home and looks for the good in every structure. Both descriptions are accurate, but the latter, this word *romantic*, gets at the emotional attachment I've felt for my personal spaces, as well as the dozens of others I've lived in vicariously during my twenty-year tenure as a shelter editor—most of it spent helming the style ship at *Garden & Gun* magazine in Charleston, South Carolina.

When I first arrived at the title (think *Vanity Fair* meets the British *House & Garden* meets *Field & Stream*), the magazine was in its infancy and it was long before we earned the Oscar of the magazine world: the coveted Ellie for General Excellence from the American Society of Magazine Editors.

When I reported for duty in July 2008, one of my first tasks was honing ideas for the style section columns. Naturally, before we talked fashion and gardens and

art and artisans, my first column idea was about houses. I told my then editor in chief, Sid Evans, that if we were going to do home stories, we needed to follow the literary bent of the rest of the magazine and make the writing about them equal to the imagery. In short, we would get at the soul. When he asked me what we should call it, I handed him a tattered copy of *A Family Place* by the Alabama writer Charles Gaines. There was something about the sentiment of the words *family* and *place* that spoke to what I meant, I told Sid. But I also knew we needed brevity, and we needed the word *home* in it. Then it came to me: *homeplace.* One word that spoke to all of it. In the years since the first iteration of our Homeplace column ran, I've tried my damnedest to seek out projects that live up to the name: family houses that spoke to specific places.

I pursued the same ideas out at home. By the time I was sitting in Sid's office, I'd already owned, renovated, and sold a house in Alabama that I polished to a shine on nights and weekends to make it my own. I hit the ground running in

Charleston, too, landing first in a historic single house (haunted!), then a charming carriage house in the Wraggborough neighborhood, and most significantly a Craftsman cottage on Grove Street off Hampton Park downtown.

This intense love for the structures we call home is a gene I inherited from my parents. They taught me to think of homes more as new friends than as jumbles of wood and metal and to design interiors and gardens in a deeply personal way, slowly and deliberately.

During the pandemic, when our family, like thousands of others, was suddenly at home a great deal, I poured myself into more painting, more planting, and more projects. Doing these things offered a salve for uncertainty—a way to insert order and beauty into life when current affairs delved into chaos. It also allowed hours of early-morning quality time with my young son, who often held a paintbrush or a water hose in his tiny hand right beside me as I worked. I don't think I'm alone with this anecdote. Across the world, families turned inward and began to think of home differently, and that hasn't waned. It's only getting stronger.

That's exactly why I set out to write this book. I want to offer a new sort of home education, one that's about surrounding yourself not with more products but with items that hold significance. Each chapter starts with a visual tour of specific areas of the Grove Street house

in Charleston that illustrate the ideals of being a house romantic—of viewing a structure as more than simply a place to fall asleep each evening. I show how these principles can be applied to other spaces, exploring how to add meaning, comfort, authenticity, flair, and references to nature, as well as the importance of carrying forward the soul of houses you've lived in. I also visit some of my design heroes from around the world, whom I call kindred spirits, as their spaces embody these notions in distinct ways. I end the chapters on what I like to call "the story behind the stuff." These are profiles on artists or artisans whose creations I love and who also work and live in inspiring spaces, revealing how understanding the human beings behind beautiful objects adds extraordinary value to our design choices.

I close the book with a dose of reality—losing the Grove Street house and moving on to another. There are many books that show only the veneer of perfection when it comes to design, that revel only in well-worn style platitudes. To me, the most important part of understanding house romanticism is knowing that it's all a bit ephemeral, that life gets messy, but continuing to look for the good in our house experiences is critical. The uglier the world seems on the outside, the more I hope readers can learn to create refuge inside, wherever that may be, for however long they call it home. ■

Opposite: Everything at the Grove Street house featured layers of storytelling, from the art to the makers behind specific pieces, right down to this ottoman by Coley Home in North Carolina.

1.

MEANING

At
Home
with
Haskell

Walls can, in fact, talk. They tell the stories of our lives. My maternal grandfather was an introspective creature. A newspaper publisher by day, he very much preferred to remain behind the photos and the headlines. This extended into his private life. I can't remember a time when he was without his Nikon. Even when he went to bed, the camera slept on his nightstand. Photography was his way of documenting the lives of his seven children without missing a moment and his armor in social settings where he acted more as party photographer than guest. I can still hear him saying, "Tell me if you're ready!" with a big grin *after* he'd already clicked the shutter, often catching his children, grandchildren, and friends in mid bite or laugh. When he passed away, one of the hardest things to divvy up into the diaspora of a giant family were the hundreds of leather-bound photo albums that filled acres of bookshelves. I have never forgotten the emotional importance of tethering a family story to the actual wood and nails and walls of a structure.

Beyond photos, my dad, also a newspaper publisher, influenced my love of collecting books and keeping only the volumes that told the world what I cared most about. To him, and now in turn to me, books are priceless possessions. He also imparted a curiosity about houses from a young age—particularly via his recollections of architectural details of his grandmother's South Carolina farm and the surrounding gardens and land. He continued this habit of telling mesmerizing house stories about all the other homes he had loved in his life throughout my childhood; he simply noticed things about physical buildings and their landscapes that other people did not. From all of this I inherited the understanding that houses were very much *alive*. Places that had a spirit in their heyday and that had the potential to live on in retellings long after the inhabitants and even the structures were gone. I never visited many of the spots he spoke about, but I feel like I did.

As a designer, my mom taught me to see the successful interiors of a house not just in the sophistication of a certain stitch or the perfect chintz but through a different type of messaging than my dad's. She possessed the imagination to memorialize and elevate inanimate objects. Examples include the piece of Tennessee pottery passed down for generations that she had wired into a showstopping lamp and the poem my nanny wrote about caring for

me as a little girl that Mom framed and gave me as a birthday gift in lieu of toys.

With both of my parents I also witnessed a great deal of sweat equity and hours of thought when it came to creating the magical laboratories for their ideas that my older brother, younger sister, and myself were lucky enough to live in and be a part of. In short, both my mom and my dad daydreamed about houses and gardens *all* the time. When they were not working, they were painting or plotting or digging out space for some new improvement. This personal devotion to reimagining, layering, and, most of all, building their lives around homes is something I absorbed through osmosis and an experience that gave my childhood homes an unusual amount of depth and purpose.

All these lessons followed me into the houses I've lived in as an adult. I bought my first home as a single twenty-five-year-old, and while it was the size of a garden shed, the project gave me a sense of empowerment and creative freedom. I was as hooked as my parents were when they took on their first crumbling, nineteen-room Georgian house as newlyweds. Then it was on to Charleston, where I eventually got married and landed in the cottage on Grove Street.

For better or for worse, I seem to be drawn to spots that need love and care. I never chose the biggest or the newest or the fanciest property in the "right" neigh-

Opposite: In the library I used an outdoor Moravian star lantern as a pendant light, a nod to memories of visiting Old Salem, a frozen-in-time eighteenth-century village down the road from my hometown growing up.

BRINGING IT ALL TOGETHER

To keep all the disparate styles of photography in the library cohesive, I printed the images in black-and-white and chose frames in chalk black, silver, and gold to impart a collected feeling. The deep blue paint on the trim, walls, baseboards, and millwork helped keep the focus on the memorabilia and the books. I had it custom mixed; after about four tries, I got it.

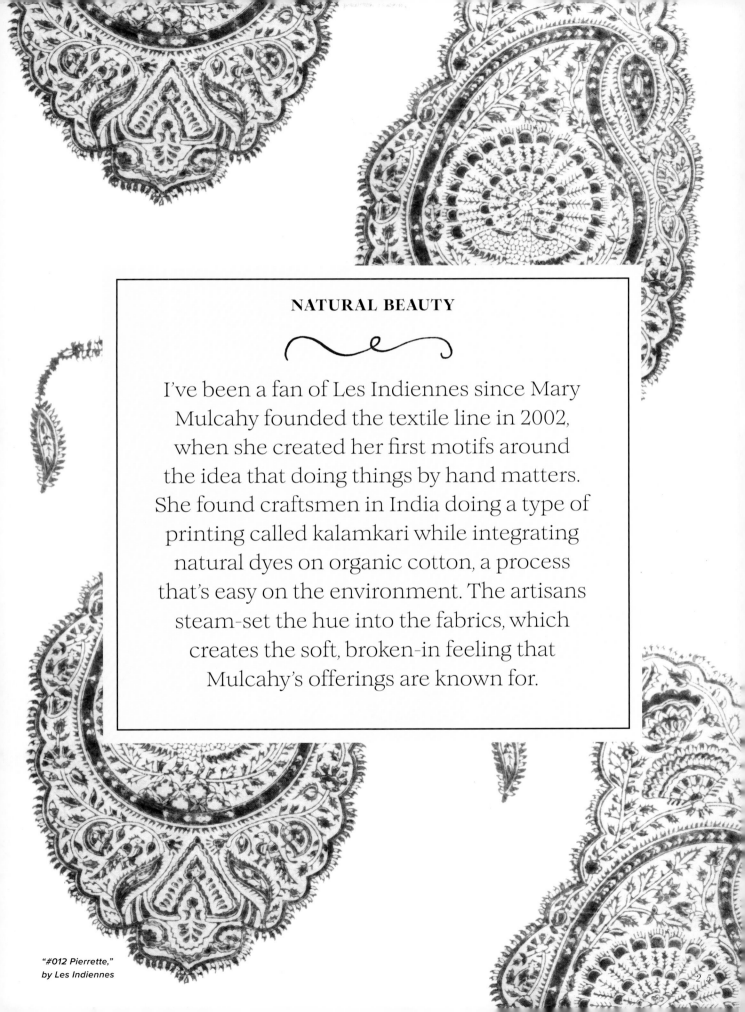

NATURAL BEAUTY

I've been a fan of Les Indiennes since Mary Mulcahy founded the textile line in 2002, when she created her first motifs around the idea that doing things by hand matters. She found craftsmen in India doing a type of printing called kalamkari while integrating natural dyes on organic cotton, a process that's easy on the environment. The artisans steam-set the hue into the fabrics, which creates the soft, broken-in feeling that Mulcahy's offerings are known for.

"#012 Pierrette,"
by Les Indiennes

A LIFE ECLECTIC

In the dining room, the mix of art
that belonged to us as a couple,
combined with the farm table I
spent many Thanksgivings around
as a child for our annual feast,
gave the whole space an especially
meaningful vibe. There is a mix
of work by photographers and
illustrators we worked with at
Garden & Gun, pedigree pieces by
artists who were close friends, and
humble sketches and scribbles by
our toddler, among other minutiae
that held significance for us and no
one else. It was a museum of our
lives and our work.

A NOTE ON MARGINALIA

mar•gi•na•li•a (noun)

*Marks made in the margins of a book or other document.
They may be scribbles, comments, glosses (annotations), critiques,
doodles, drolleries, or illuminations. (Wikipedia)*

I am a huge fan of putting things that
matter out in the open, so tucking a poem
or a photo or a postcard into the frame of
our dining room mirror became something
of a sport over time. This gesture and other
similar ones have felt like the notes
in the margins of life.

Opposite: "Mizu" linen, by Studio Four NYC

borhood, and that was deliberate. Before my paintbrush ever touched a wall, I saw that these diminutive spaces had something interesting to say if the right caretaker came along. And I tried to be that person for the limited amount of time I spent living in them.

One of the best tricks to conjuring meaning inside these abodes happens in the editing and the display. It isn't about the volume of things, but the essence of very specific art and books and heirlooms. And it doesn't have to involve some sort of brutal culling, but simply taking an inventory of items that bring positive emotions to the surface, such as grounding feelings like contentment or confidence or connection.

In the Grove Street house, I spent hours narrowing down photos from generations of my family and my husband's family to frame and hang in the library, an ideal spot for a bit of reflection. I felt like concentrating everything in this one space rather than scattering frames in every room not only helped with clutter, but added more interest, too. I decided on pairings like our childhood photos hung side by side; portraits of our grandmothers, who were formative in our lives; our wedding photo; images from our parents and their childhoods; and more modern portraits. I also framed important letters, invitations, and other family pieces that might otherwise be relegated to the attic. In the process, the

space morphed into a giant scrapbook to pore over any time we or our friends felt like it. It also became the main hub for our book collection.

Similarly, the family and dining rooms of Grove Street operated as a gallery for pieces of family art collected intentionally over time to canvas every inch of space in both rooms. Art is always in the eye of the beholder and can include not only pedigree pieces but the humble and the personal, too, from a framed abstract in crayon by our toddler to mounted textiles gathered during travel to architectural remnants and more.

On Grove Street and in every other home I've lived in, the objects—the furniture, the lighting, and even the accessories—also symbolize far more than their utilitarian purpose. As a style editor, I've seen so many homes that are thrillingly beautiful, but the ones that stick with me most (and with readers) are the ones that feel personal. That's because you don't have to look at what someone else is doing to dream up a remarkable space. The real path to originality is shining a spotlight on your life.

In this chapter, we'll visit the interior designer Angie Hranowsky, the Texas shop owner and international vagabond Courtney Barton, and the antiquarian Ajiri Aki of Madame de la Maison, who all bring their own versions of meaning into their homes in one-of-a-kind ways.

Opposite: On Grove Street I corralled all things bar into a glass-fronted cabinet. Truly any corner or surface or area can be turned into a libation station.

3 0

A chair from my childhood bedroom forms the perfect perch for some favorite design reads.

"One of the best tricks to *conjuring meaning* inside these abodes and any others, at least to me, happens in the editing and the display. It isn't about the volume of things, but the *significance* of very specific art and books and heirlooms."

THE TINY ARTIST

When he was a baby, one of my little boy's favorite things to scribble on was a cardboard box. One afternoon, while we were waiting for a hurricane to pass outside the front door, he scribbled a masterpiece, and I sat on the floor and doodled, too. Later, as I was about to recycle it all, I cut this piece of the box out and had it framed. There are so many wonderful mail-order framing resources now that make this idea a cinch (see page 265).

Opposite: "Petite Zoebel" linen, by Wayne Pate + Studio Four NYC

Angie at home in
front of a painting
by P. R. McIntosh

Angie Hranowsky

Charleston, South Carolina

I met Angie Hranowsky years ago, when I first moved to Charleston, and loved her from the start, both as an interior designer and as a person. I was in awe of her talent and admired her caring and cosmopolitan nature . . . and she laughed at my jokes. As our friendship deepened, I also developed a respect for the ways in which she showed up for every important person in her life, including me.

These qualities appear in her work, too, if you pay attention. In her new (very dreamy) personal house, which she built from scratch out of Carolina cypress, the tableau of every room presents an aesthetic feast that brings the people and places of her life into living color.

I notice different things each time I spend time there, but I've always been drawn to her jewelry and ceramics. Unlike some designers who might tuck these items out of view, Angie uses them to enrich the rooms where she displays them.

I'm intrigued by her jewelry collection because Angie has an understated, French way of wearing things. Her pieces are not trendy; they are her talismans and her trademarks. My favorite is her gold Omega watch, which belonged to her paternal grandfather; she had it refitted to her wrist. "I am an only child, and my dad was an only child and he passed away when I was six, so I was also the only grandchild, and when my grandparents passed away, I inherited all their jewelry," she says. "I'm not one to wear a lot of different things and I've always worn pieces that are personal to me."

She keeps everything in beautiful containers in her bedroom. The vessels hold prized pieces, like the monogrammed gold heart locket that belonged to Angie's grandmother that Angie wore on her wedding day, a sterling silver cuff from the South of France that was a gift from Angie's mom, and even a new addition

The dressing area in Angie's bedroom, replete with her jewelry collection

Clockwise from top left:

*Never-ending art and
ceramics; heirloom jewelry
with the loveliest stories;
Rocco the cat; and fresh,
Seuss-ical flowers are
all beautiful reasons I love
visiting Angie at home.*

of stacking rings Angie commissioned to be handmade by a designer in Maine. "I just like to style things so I get to see all of the meaningful pieces," she says. "It's personal, but it's also a form of design."

This wild, colorful environment where she chooses what she will wear each day is akin to getting dressed in an other-worldly paradise. "I knew when I built the house that I wanted my bedroom to be an enveloping extension of the bamboo and banana trees outside my windows," she says. After looking for the right print for months and even considering a mural, Angie fell in love with a kaleidoscopic collaboration between Voutsa and CW Stockwell—so much so that she not only used the wallpaper but also continued with the same print for the drapery panels. "I wanted the pattern to wrap the room to make it seamless," she says.

Other vignettes in the house bring her pottery and books into focus. In one area, Angie clustered several vases and bowls together that illustrate the breadth of time periods evident in her ceramics. "I started collecting in my twenties at flea markets," she says. "I've refined my eye since then, and now I try to only invest in pieces that I really love." Books are another weakness for Angie, thanks to her former career as a graphic designer. "Books bring so much life and art to a space," she says. "Just seeing them stacked around the house can inspire your children to be curious and to wonder at what might be inside." Some-

times Angie will also buy books for their thoughtful aesthetics. "I love book covers and book jackets. It's all art, the book design, the cover art, the typography, the writing, all of it." I vividly recall Angie shipping herself a huge box of beautiful books—all in Spanish—from her last Mexico adventure.

It all works and doesn't slip into the sweet or the saccharine thanks to additions that bring a sense of erudition. Case in point: the thorn mirror she purchased from the American expat, artist, and antiques dealer Mike Diaz after visiting his studio in Mexico City. "I remember ending up at this beautiful old house that was full of Mexican and European antiques mixed with modern furniture as well as his pieces and being really moved," she says. Angie bought one of his mirrors and saved it for the perfect moment to hang it when her new house was complete. She is very patient, and good things come to those who savor each new addition.

But her true gift is being able to curate spaces for her clients that feel just as narrated. "I love a home that piques my interest and makes me ask, *What's their story? Where have they traveled? What are their passions in life?*" she says, adding, "I think the same can be true for homes that are professionally designed. It's all in how you personalize it to feel distinctive to its inhabitants." ∎

Opposite: At Angie's house, there are always new arrangements capped off by stunning objects like this lamp by Matthias Vriens.

VOGUE'S BOOK OF ETIQUETTE

INTERIORS

Make It Fabulous

DIAZ-AZCUY

ART ASSOULINE

Galerie Jacques Lacoste
Galerie Patrick Seguin

ASSOULINE

Dara Caponigro

A mirror by artist Mike Diaz anchors one of Angie's showstopping vignettes.

"Books bring *so much life* and art to a space. Just seeing them stacked around the house can inspire your children to be curious and to wonder at what might be inside."

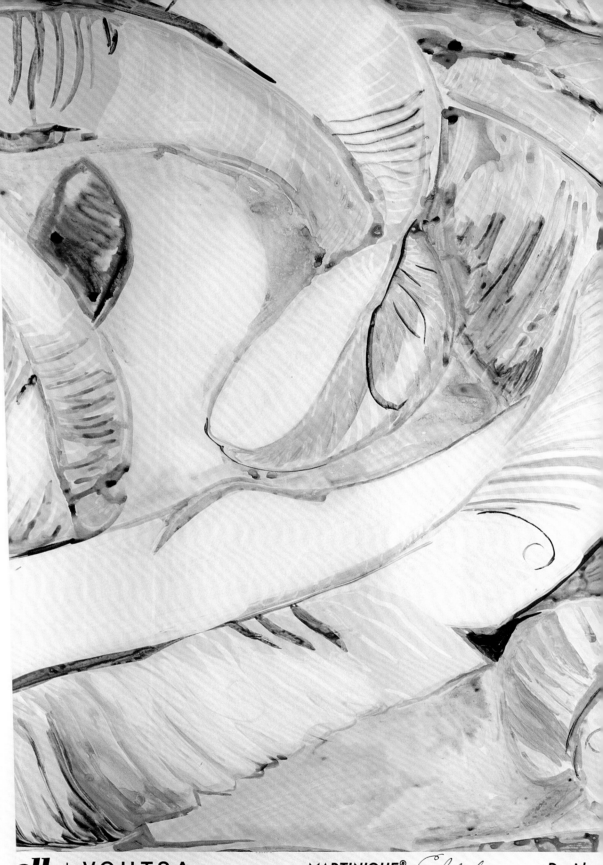

ell + VOUTSA   MARTINIQUE® *Celebration*   **David**

"David" linen, by CW Stockwell x Voutsa Martinique© Celebration!

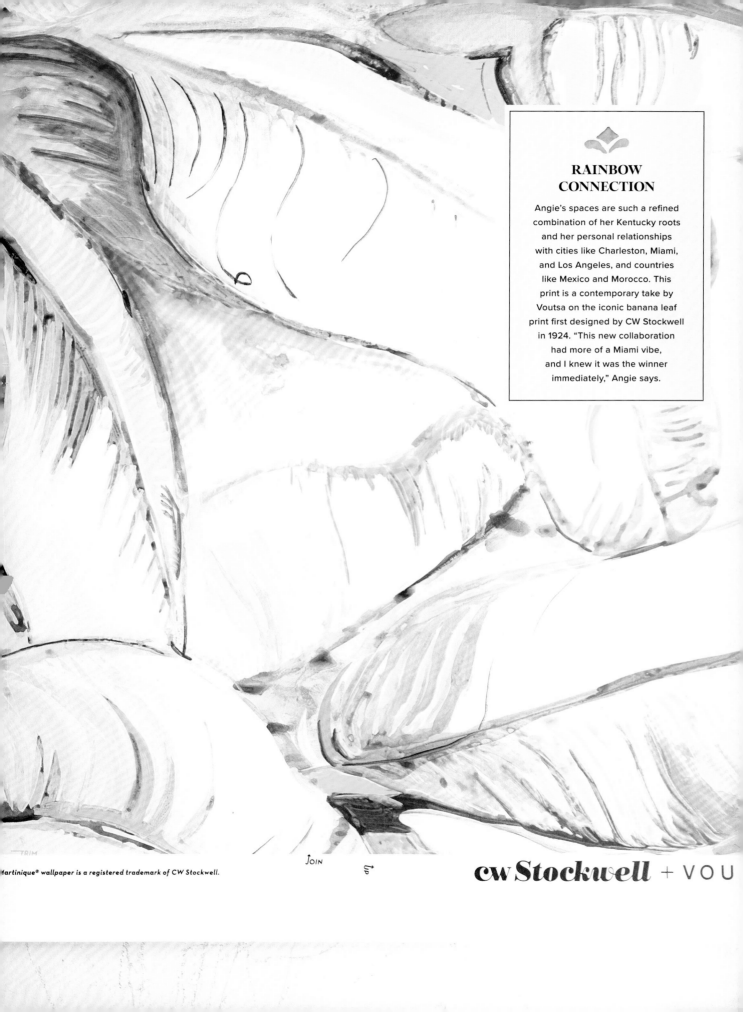

RAINBOW CONNECTION

Angie's spaces are such a refined combination of her Kentucky roots and her personal relationships with cities like Charleston, Miami, and Los Angeles, and countries like Mexico and Morocco. This print is a contemporary take by Voutsa on the iconic banana leaf print first designed by CW Stockwell in 1924. "This new collaboration had more of a Miami vibe, and I knew it was the winner immediately," Angie says.

TRIM

JOIN

UP

Martinique® wallpaper is a registered trademark of CW Stockwell.

cw Stockwell + VOU

Courtney's guest bedroom is a lesson in layering textiles, from the monogrammed pillowcases to the antique quilt.

Courtney Barton

Houston, Texas

One of the most tried-and-true ways to add substance to a house is via the magic of objects collected on adventures around the world. It's an art form that the textile designer and shop owner Courtney Barton has spent her adult life perfecting.

She says it all started with a fateful move to Malaysia with her husband in 2009 after a stint in the fashion world working for Ralph Rucci and Jill Stuart. "It was during this expat season that I began collaborating with artisans I met during my travels to design home goods. I amassed a collection of antique linens and other exotic finds, so my business grew organically," she says.

Over the years Courtney set up shop first in Houston and most recently in the worldwide mecca for antiques and interesting finds: Round Top, Texas. Both locales are slightly different in their offerings, but they have a common thread in

the textiles Courtney designs alongside artisans in Rajasthan, India, and sells in her stores.

These soft, subtle creations are the reason I know Courtney. Years ago, she sent a sample of a dohar she designed so that I could see and feel it in person. At the time, I was unaware of the long history of this uniquely Indian blanket. Her take on the idea involved layers of combed cotton—all block printed by hand with motifs she drew and had dyed with the gentle colors she's now known for. To me, the dohar fell somewhere between a gauze coverlet and a quilt and felt as suited to a humid Southern summer as it did a sweltering Indian one. There was something familiar about it, as if it bridged two cultures.

And it is perhaps the staggering combination of both vintage and modern textiles inside Courtney's home that most clearly tells of her vagabond wanderings.

Opposite: In the dining room, Courtney tempered the older pieces with modern dining chairs.

This page: Courtney's self-described "cabinet of curiosities" in the kitchen includes bits and bobs from all her travels that she uses every day.

Courtney paid homage to her most recent trip to India by framing a piece of a lyrical painting called a pichwai and hanging it in the family room.

This page: Courtney's scouring trips also include regular visits to South Louisiana, where she found this trombone light.

Opposite: A camel saddlebag from Fez and a vintage Indian bandhani wool wedding shawl are two beloved textile souvenirs from recent jaunts.

TRAVEL AS AUTOBIOGRAPHY

One takeaway from Courtney's aesthetic is the importance of close observation while traveling and bringing back bits of this and that to recall the human beings behind the artistry from all over the world. Even if you just head out for the weekend somewhere close by, seek out artisans to support and bring their work home. Their story then becomes part of yours.

Courtney purchased this giant riff on a tree of life, Oh to Be Fed, by Louisiana artist Rebecca Rebouche, for her husband on their tenth wedding anniversary.

"Handmade products bear the marks of the artists, leaving no two alike," she says. This devotion to soft goods is no doubt influenced by her French Acadian grand-mother, who instilled an early love of items made by hand. "She embroidered and monogrammed every tea towel and bed linen," Courtney remembers. "And I use many of these same textiles in my house today and am so inspired by their lasting impact."

Beyond just textiles, the way in which Courtney combines her heirloom pieces with more modern additions of her own is also delightful. It's a wonderful contrast to see an antique lamp base Courtney found on a trip to China topped off with a shade made from one of her printed cotton fabrics, for example. There simply isn't a room in her home where these seemingly opposing ideas don't live in beautiful harmony. Courtney's uncle, an antiques dealer, used to ask her, "Do you love it? Do you find value in it?" when she called for advice on buying trips. "I still abide by this code, and it's never led me astray," she says.

Even the colors chosen for her home stem from experiences abroad. The peachy pink of her living room is pulled directly from an ancient oil painting she discovered at a market in India that hangs near the fireplace. The chalky brown-gray in her dining room is the precise color of the artful wooden blocks used to put ink to cotton for her fabrics. "I still find myself in constant amazement of the unforgettable sights I've seen and the people I've met," she says. "I've witnessed every extreme imaginable, both high and low, and I'm better for it."

Courtney will be jet-setting into more collaborations soon. The first will be a range of bespoke quilts, created in tandem with her artisan team in India. "I want the pieces to speak to the heart and reflect that same enthusiasm in a space."

"In France, the process of taking small items of personal importance—like shells, crockery, and buttons—and embedding them in putty is called pique assiette," Courtney says of this antique lamp base.

"HANDMADE PRODUCTS BEAR THE MARKS OF THE ARTISTS, LEAVING NO TWO ALIKE."

THE STORY BEHIND THE STUFF

Vintage Tableware

by Ajiri Aki of Madame de la Maison, Paris, France

Many years ago, I took a brief hiatus from magazines and worked in the event-design business in Charleston. One thing I observed in that world, at least in the United States, is that most stemware and tabletop sourced for high-end events is rented and new. It makes sense from a practical standpoint, but I felt that these one-of-a-kind parties lacked that extra layer of something old, something with history.

So when I first learned about the Texan expat Ajiri Aki and her Paris-based business, Madame de la Maison, where she curates events with vintage tableware and runs a retail site for purchasing these special items, I was smitten. Not only because she has beautiful taste and a staggering knowledge of provenance, but also because she is such a force in the way that she styles her entire life, right down to her signature bright lip and enviable jewelry collection.

When I visited her in Paris, the enchantment continued as I learned more about the influence of her Nigerian-born mother. "My mother was absolutely the force in my childhood that sparked my love of objects," Ajiri says. "She would take me to garage sales in Austin, and there was something fascinating to me about a person looking through piles of unwanted objects and that person, the searcher, having the sensibility to know that this object has further use." Her mother also created ceramics and placed them around the house, a practice that inspired Ajiri. "The fact that she displayed something that she found beautiful intrigued me then and inspires me today."

After her childhood in Texas, Ajiri found herself in the editorial sphere, working for the likes of *W*, *Suede*, *Nylon*, and *Interview*, soon followed by a stint at the Costume Institute at the Metropolitan Museum of Art. At the same time,

Ajiri wearing her trademark rings and bangles, holding one of the many antique coupes in her personal collection

*This page and opposite:
The dining room of Ajiri's
Paris apartment serves
as an ever-changing set
and entertaining venue
for her family, her friends,
and her business,
Madame de la Maison.*

Ajiri's striped pieces are thirties art deco designs made in Sarreguemines, France, a region where ceramics have been produced since the eighteenth century.

"[My mother] would take me to garage sales in Austin, and there was something fascinating to me about a person looking through piles of tables of unwanted objects and that person, the searcher, having the sensibility to know that *this* object has further use."

she pursued a graduate degree at Bard College. "I loved working in fashion but ultimately realized I was more interested in history and stories that inspired many of the shoots I worked on," she says of the switch. Ajiri soon found herself in Paris researching a thesis on Jean Patou, a fateful trip that led to her meeting her Swiss German husband and settling down permanently in France.

Entertaining became Ajiri's way of making new friends, and she approached it like a Texan: with open arms. "I feel the world of entertaining can be exclusive and prohibitive," she says. "A lot of it focuses on perfection and rules. When I came to France to find a community, I did this while ignoring all that. I did things my own way and developed a reputation as a hostess of gatherings that people remembered and truly enjoyed."

This realization led to Ajiri founding Madame de la Maison in 2018. "I want to be a model of joy for my children, as my mother was for me," she says. "I want them to understand and *feel* the fellowship of gathering around a table." And even though Texas is thousands of miles away and Ajiri can't attend Sunday suppers with her own family in Austin, she's created new traditions abroad and is honoring that bond with her business.

To find the exquisite crystal, silver, and gold vermeil vessels and vintage linens, Ajiri travels across France three times a year. "On a daily basis, I encounter people who have an appreciation and deep love of history and the decorative arts and overall," she says. "The French possess an appreciation of history and beauty found in objects of the past, and bringing them into modern-day life, that's very different from where I grew up, where the focus is on everything that's new." Recently, Ajiri expanded her searches beyond just tabletop to mirrors, books, and decorative items. And her fifth-floor apartment in the fourteenth arrondissement is an ever-shifting photo shoot set for all her finds.

And while Ajiri is continually enamored of the way the French approach the celebration of daily life, a more laid-back approach inspired by Texas hospitality is never far from her mind when she's hosting friends old and new. "I absolutely infuse that 'everything is bigger in Texas' notion into what I do with my business and how I receive people," she says. "That Southern sentiment that one's door is always open is not French at all, but my French doors are always open. As for my table styling, while the French might keep their table simple, I like adding all the extra bits and maybe being a bit over-the-top."

I hope Ajiri will continue seeking out all those special things for a long time to come so that the rest of us can enjoy her eye and her edit. ◾

Clockwise from top left:

Ajiri on her Parisian balcony; her bar; a vintage hand-painted Quimper plate; her treasure trove of crystal

2.

COMFORT

At Home
with
Haskell

I am a believer that comfort isn't a form of indulgence; it's an essential element for health and well-being. And for as long as I can remember, the places I've lived have provided a sanctuary of sensory sustenance. It isn't about decorating. It isn't about doing this or that "right." It's more wrapped up in the idea of nurturing yourself first and then the people who pass through your doors. As I write these words, I'm surrounded by things that bring me solace. I'm sitting at my desk with a weighted blanket on my lap, a pot of Earl Grey tea, a white noise machine going, a little potted cyclamen to look at when I need a break, and a few things simmering on the stove so the whole house smells wonderful. Oh, and I have a fire going in the living room.

I knew as a child, and especially now as an adult, that my ability to thrive involves feeding all five senses in this way. At my current age of forty-three, this might seem normal. In my younger years, not so much. When I moved into my first apartment at the University of Virginia, my roommates teased me endlessly about all my bathrobes and pillows and flowers and books and how I loved to cook. I guess it seemed out of step with other bacchanalian pursuits of our college lives (though I imbibed in all those as well).

Later, after I purchased my first house, I grew to appreciate my quirky old-soulness about creature comforts and not to see it as some sort of character flaw. At age twenty-five, it brought me a great deal of joy in my house in Alabama to create pockets of beauty with ordinary objects. Something as humble as storing whole coffee beans in a giant apothecary jar transformed my mornings into meditations. I could see it, smell it, touch it, listen to it brewing, and then taste it, too.

On Grove Street, my love of soft blankets and bedding and down-filled everything continued. I got funny looks from the wonderful upholstery artisans who rebuilt the living room sofa when I asked to add down feather beds to layer on top of the standard sofa cushions. It all blended together and added an extra layer of fluff. My request paid off every single time I napped on those feather beds or watched movies with my little boy. And the real bonus? I could easily unzip the covers, wash them, fluff them all up, and sink in all over again.

In the primary bedroom, I researched the exact coverlets and mattress used at the Hotel Amparo in San Miguel de Allende in Mexico, an oasis where I once recovered from food poisoning and entirely credit the good night's sleep I experienced there for healing me. I also stocked every bathroom with too many towels and nearly every room with washable cotton throw blankets in baskets, just because.

More than simply collecting objects of tactile softness, the idea of comfort, at least in the nests I've feathered, filters into other things, too. Bookshelves filled to the brim with interesting cookbooks and design books and family albums create a cocoon of familiarity and warmth and plenty. Other seemingly little things do, too: A full fruit bowl. Colors that lift spirits. A stocked bar. Little clippings of yard flowers tucked on windowsills and bedside tables. Music playing that feels just right for a particular moment. Or no music at all, just the bliss of peace and quiet. And always lots of lotions and potions and lovely little apothecary items to enjoy in the kitchen and laundry and bathrooms. All of these ideas, and my knowledge and enjoyment of them, are directly related to my mom focusing on the same things. I still tell friends who haven't met her yet (because it sums her up perfectly) that she often brings her own pillows, sheets, and snacks to hotel rooms to make them feel more like home. I guess it's with my parents that my idea of a house as a place of respite from the outside world rests.

I also visited a home often in high school that belonged to my best friend at the time that stuck with me. It was different than the houses that I knew from living with my family because it was very casual and dressed down in comparison to the starched and elegant rooms my mom designed. At my best friend's

Opposite: I try to keep comforting things in rotation at home that stimulate all five senses. A single-serve teapot and surrounding myself with cookbooks and design books are go-to self-care moves.

der, house building is "both a[...]
start." In his wonderful book *F[...]
for the New World Puritan [...]
religious transfiguration, a god[...]
godly handiwork in which the [...]
the bones, the clapboards skin, [...]
eyes, and the door a mouth. "[...]
quotes folklorist Robert St. Ge[...]
effort to stop time, suspend d[...]
flow to ruin that started with [...]
quotes Mircea Eliade, the great [...]
calls home construction " 'a ne[...]
life.' "

In fact, until you do it yo[...]
godlike and exhilarating it does[...]
hands and tools to build a ho[...]
family—particularly when scra[...]
between you and the weather. [...]

The reorganization of our [...]

Down feather beds on the sofa, extra pillows, a soft rug underfoot, happy color and pattern, lots of good books, and yard flowers are all small but mighty comforts in the living room on Grove Street.

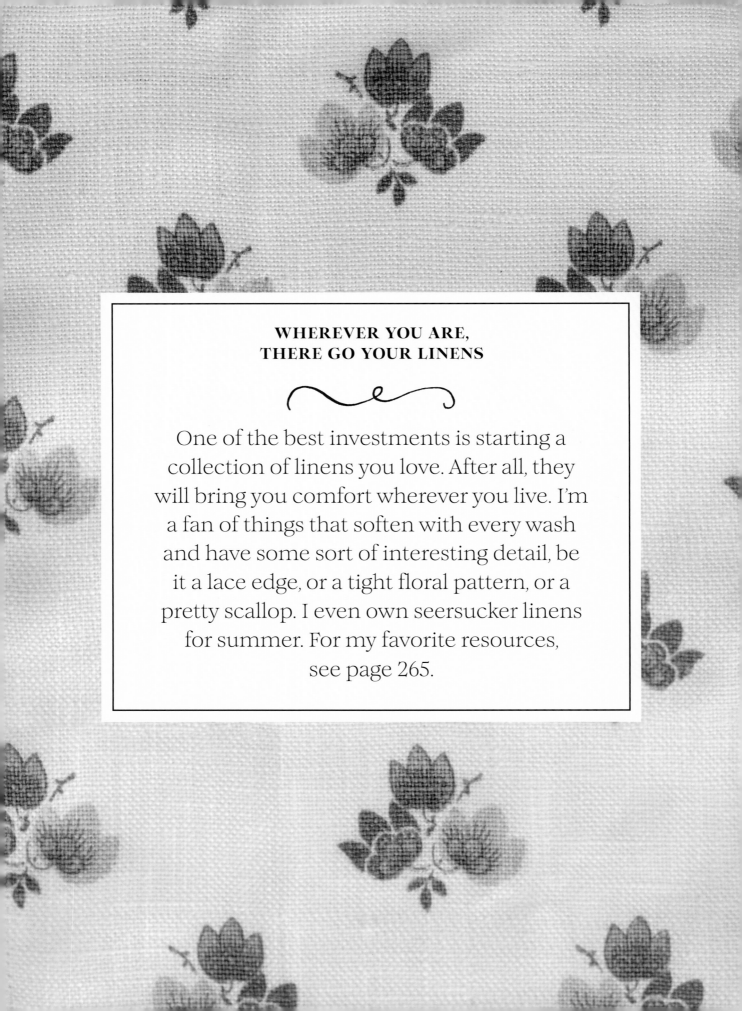

WHEREVER YOU ARE,
THERE GO YOUR LINENS

One of the best investments is starting a collection of linens you love. After all, they will bring you comfort wherever you live. I'm a fan of things that soften with every wash and have some sort of interesting detail, be it a lace edge, or a tight floral pattern, or a pretty scallop. I even own seersucker linens for summer. For my favorite resources, see page 265.

Opposite: "Beatrice," by Alice Sergeant Textiles

This page: I commissioned built-ins to the primary bedroom on Grove Street for linens.

The primary bed is the work of craftsman Andrew Reid in Alabama. For added comfort I included a featherbed and soft layers of textiles gathered on trips to Mexico and beyond.

"A home is meant
to be a spot where
the brain and
the body are able
to *recoup energy*
for the next day
in the world."

house, there was always something baking in the oven, all the bedding was over-washed, and there was a calming order and fresh-scrubbed but faded and well-loved feeling about it that felt restorative. I've borrowed heavily from the time I spent in that space, too, as an adult.

What they all had in common was the idea that a home is meant to be a spot where the brain and the body are able to *recoup energy* for the next day in the world. Perhaps no other time in history demonstrated this quite so acutely as the pandemic did. Suddenly, human beings began thinking of their spaces completely differently. Some took down an old cookbook from the shelf and used a recipe from it rather than staring at one on a screen. Some set elaborate tables to celebrate another Tuesday gone by. Some made a lot of sourdough. And home felt like the safest place on Earth on a few of those weird days.

In this chapter, we'll visit three of my favorite style arbiters who also happen to be experts in the comfort department. I often look to their work for even more ways to bring a sense of peace and ease home. First up is the chic and womb-like abode of the interior designer Victoria Sass in Minneapolis, Minnesota; then we take a jaunt across the pond to the dopamine-decorated home of the British interior designer Lizzie Green; and we return back to the States to a modern surf shack owned by the designer and hotelier Kate Towill and her family on the Isle of Palms in South Carolina. Finally, we stop in Laurel Canyon in Los Angeles to catch up with the designer Heather Taylor, whose eponymous line of table linens, bedding, and cushy upholstered furniture are all illustrative of the precise forms of sensory pleasure that are so central to being a house romantic. ▪

Clockwise from top left:

Beach bags and hats at the ready for boat days; one of my favorite (and softest) pillows by Archive New York; lively paper flowers by Livia Cetti; Auggie on the sofa's featherbed cushions

Victoria Sass

Minneapolis, Minnesota

Until I met the Minneapolis, Minnesota, interior designer Victoria Sass in person, I didn't realize how much the Midwest and the South have in common—namely the ability to make anyone feel well-fed and welcome. Within moments of entering her front door, there were hugs and offers of tea and coffee and breakfast and a general air of excitement about sharing her home. No ego, no pretension. All of this makes sense, of course, because Victoria's work communicates the same experience. Is it stylish, forward-thinking, and sophisticated? Yes, but the sinews holding it together are caring and curiosity for and about people.

"I get a lot of pleasure out of people's personalities and enjoy bringing out the magic that objects possess—my career is a perfect marriage of those two loves," Victoria says of her eight-year-old firm Prospect Refuge, which fittingly began as a ceramics studio with a friend and eventually morphed into her going out on her own.

Her current house is emblematic of this idea of nurturing people, of helping clients surround themselves and their families with items that bring comfort and contentment and beauty. "I had just forbidden my husband from looking at any more homes," she remembers of the moment she found it. "I settled my mind that we were just going to stay put, so, of course, I immediately came upon this home and had to go to him and eat crow. It has a little bit of elbow room, good bones, lots of quirk, and enough projects to keep us busy dreaming for a lifetime together."

Like many homes in the neighborhood and in Minneapolis in general, it hails from the early twentieth century—a time when the area experienced a surge of prosperity and residential building. Built

The open pantry and veritable hothouse of plants in every nook in Victoria's kitchen are instantly inviting.

around 1900 as a suburban farmhouse, it was later carved up into three separate residences. "Our first order of business was to finish transforming it back into a single-family home, so we opened up and reorganized the back half of the main floor into a more open room," says Victoria. "I have lots of little kids so I wanted one place where we could all be together, even if we were doing separate things."

In contrast to this idea of close proximity to family life, Victoria eventually transformed a catchall space in the center of the first floor into a full-time office that feels completely her own. It's a chic cocoon of things that inspire her, from books and objects to the wallpaper and fabric by Nicholas Herbert called Toile des Lapins that cloak every visible surface. "I call it my little butter pat," Victoria says. "It's transportive and insulated at the same time so I feel like I am in my own little world and can really focus."

Meanwhile, in some of the more formal front rooms, Victoria lightened the serious architectural mood with a fabric called Les Groseilles by Décors Barbares on the walls of the entry and having her friends Kate Worum and Jennifer Jorgensen, the artists from She She, hand-paint the parlor with a swirling avian motif. "Sometimes you just have to put big personalities next to big personalities to give it all a sense of proportion," she says. "I think a space that has a lot going on can absorb the chaos of everyday life a little better."

Victoria also brought in softness throughout the house wherever possible with layers of interesting textiles: throw pillows downstairs by all sorts of wonderful designers, laid-back bedding, and tablecloths in myriad ways. "I'm a big fan of using playful pieces as a way to soften or shape the energy of a space without making a big commitment. Tablecloths are my absolute favorite. They are so useful: Tuck one around the seat cushions on your sofa, drape one over a sideboard, pin one up in front of your dysfunctional fireplace, the list goes on and on." This natural instinct for smoothing hard edges and creating a sense of escape and safety is one that Victoria attributes to her mother. "She has a way of making simple things so cozy. She just takes whatever is around her and loves it up and makes it special."

This attention to sensory details, the seeing, hearing, touching, tasting, smelling parts of the house—right down to her teacups by Ginny Sims, her supply of halva (a favorite snack to enjoy with cheese and fruit), and incense she makes herself after learning at the High Desert Observatory—creates a sense that Victoria lives as she's always lived, bringing presence and pleasure to the everyday. She says, "It's that process of learning about what people are really searching for in life—be it connection or seclusion, abundance or reduction, activity or rest—that is our true work." ∎

Opposite: Victoria cloaked her office in "Toile de Lapins," by Nicholas Herbert, right down to drapery panels embellishing her bookshelves.

I was completely
beguiled by the contrasts
in Victoria's spaces,
especially in the way that
she combined more classic
elements like checks
and quilted textures
with such incredibly airy,
modern silhouettes.

DO WHATEVER
YOU WANT
NO ONE GIVES

SOFTENING A SPACE WITH TEXTILES

"I'm a big fan of using playful pieces as
a way to soften or shape the energy of a
space without making a big commitment.
Tablecloths are my absolute favorite. They
are so useful: Tuck one around the seat
cushions on your sofa, drape one over
a sideboard, pin one up in front of your
dysfunctional fireplace, the list goes on
and on."

Opposite: *"Rainbow Rose," by House of Hackney*

This page: A nonworking fireplace in the primary bedroom gets a glamorous custom panel.

Victoria lightened the heavy paneling of the original house with ebullient textiles.

Clockwise from top left:

A casual tablecloth in the formal dining room perfectly merges opposite ideas; wallpaper envelopes the powder room; the primary bedroom features layered bedding and cozy drapery panels; faux-mink slides by Suzanne Rae

The breakfast area in Victoria's house is yet another spot where she uses textiles to brighten a space and allay hard surfaces.

"Sometimes you just have to put big personalities next to big personalities to give it all a sense of proportion. I think a space that has a lot going on can absorb the chaos of everyday life a little better."

Lizzie Green at home in the nursery painted by artist Queenie Ingrams to welcome the arrival of Lizzie's first baby

Lizzie Green

London, England

When I had my little boy, my aesthetic profoundly changed. After years of living in homes with layered neutrals, I was suddenly drawn to confetti colors. Having a child reinvigorated my sense of wonder again, and I wanted to create an environment that provided fuel for his imagination. What I found in the process is that color isn't just a decorative element. Color *is* comfort; it's a mood booster and a balm to children and adults alike. There is something about a bright, impish hue that has the capacity to jolt a person back into a sated, glass-half-full outlook. The same can be said for healthy doses of the whimsy and humor designing a home with a child (or a child at heart) living in it inevitably brings. I think that's why I found myself drawn to the work of British interior designer and fellow mother Lizzie Green.

Her first project that stopped me in my tracks featured a stately Georgian town-house in London with five central staircases embellished with a sunshine-yellow runner. Fun, surprising, and yes, childlike, but not *childish*. A single color conveyed a comforting sense of immediate joy—like feeling warm sun on your face in the middle of winter. I loved it.

So it seems fitting that when I met Lizzie for the first time, she was holding her firstborn, then four-week-old Leo. Also fitting: Inside the 1896 brick Victorian terrace in London she shares with her young family, the first room completed in the top-to-bottom renovation was the nursery. Every surface features the kaleidoscopic work of the English muralist Queenie Ingrams and her take on Beatrix Potter characters. Hither and thither you'll find Jemima Puddle-Duck, Peter Rabbit, and all the rest peeking out from swaying wildflowers and tufts of grass. "I love working with playful palettes, color blocking, clean design, unexpected ele-

Opposite: *Lizzie's interiors, including her new kitchen, are comforting in their cheerful use of bright color in places that are in use every day.*

This page: Lizzie's collection of Polaroids documents all the visits from friends and family with her newborn.

Carving out
intentional areas
for refuge are
also hallmarks of
Lizzie's look.

"Color is uplifting and makes you feel pleased to be there and adds such a unique sense of character to the room."

ments, and blends of old and new," Lizzie says, "and I try to reject rigid rules."

The rest of the house needed this lively touch, too. Nestled in Nunhead, a neighborhood in South East London that was once replete with small farms growing produce before population growth initiated a boom in Victorian residential and commercial buildings, the structure featured the solid construction Lizzie and her husband were after. "The proportions of the house are great with lovely-sized rooms and high ceilings," she says. "It was also a total mess, but I loved that it felt like a completely blank canvas, allowing us to rearrange the rooms for modern living, all within the brick walls of a well-built home."

To brighten the traditionally dark entry, kitchen, and front sitting room of the house, which gets very little natural light, Lizzie not only extended the entire back of the house and added skylights but injected the kitchen with a wallop of bright cornflower-blue paint on the cabinetry. "I wanted the space to feel open and comfortable with lots of different zones to relax," she says. "That color is uplifting and makes you feel pleased to be there and adds such a unique sense of character to the room." Lizzie also added ample display space in the kitchen for all the things she loves, including art scored on a trip across the English Channel to Paris and her collection of ceramics, glassware, and cookbooks.

And because Lizzie likes to call attention to architectural details in her work, she stripped layers of old paint off the original treads on the staircase leading to the second floor and layered on a graphic stripe. Even the upstairs bathroom went through a cheerful metamorphosis in the form of a pink tub and open shelving for everything from soaps and all things apothecary and self-care to other curiosities. "I don't like to make bathrooms clinical," she says.

Downstairs in the front sitting room, Lizzie softened the bay window with a bright, rainbow-hued floral drapery treatment sewn by her mother that brings a bit of the garden and farming history of the area indoors. "My mum is a curtain maker and has been for thirty years, so I have a passion for beautiful fabrics and drapery," Lizzie says. "To me a room feels unfinished until the curtains are hung. Especially here, we need to bring warmth to our homes."

And the house certainly has warmth in spades. ◼

Opposite: Relaxed furniture punctuated by graphic patterns fills the living room—where Lizzie's new baby often naps in his wicker bassinet—with a youthful, comforting vibe.

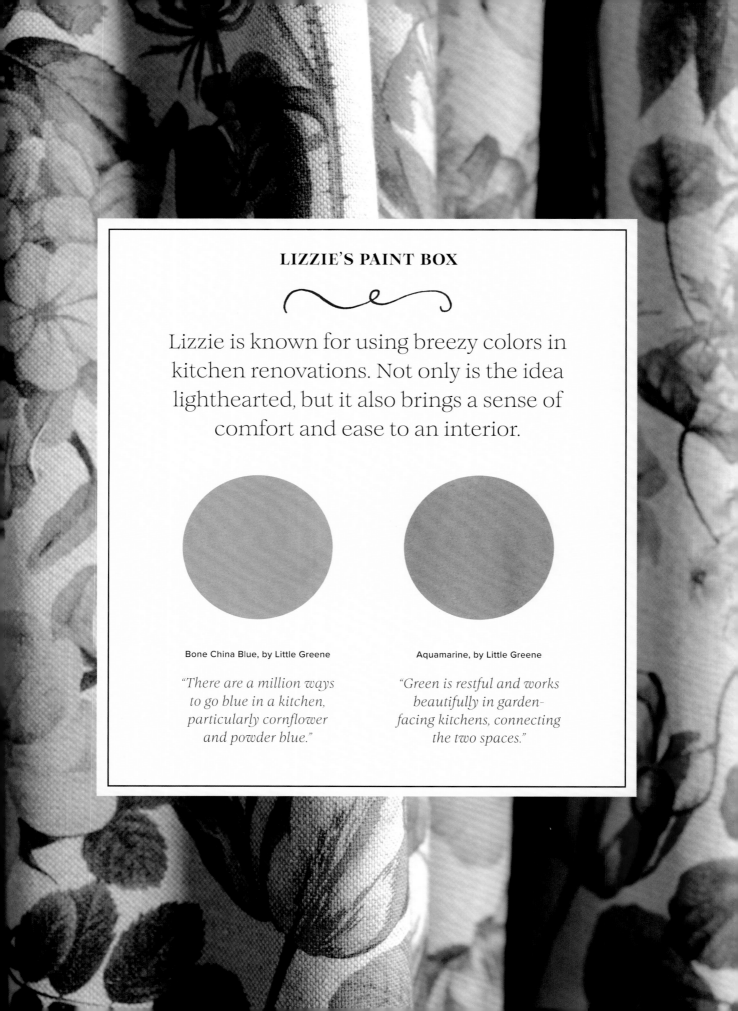

LIZZIE'S PAINT BOX

Lizzie is known for using breezy colors in kitchen renovations. Not only is the idea lighthearted, but it also brings a sense of comfort and ease to an interior.

Bone China Blue, by Little Greene

"There are a million ways to go blue in a kitchen, particularly cornflower and powder blue."

Aquamarine, by Little Greene

"Green is restful and works beautifully in garden-facing kitchens, connecting the two spaces."

*This page: Lizzie specified a striped staircase leading to the
second floor, a move that creates a joyful focal point.*

Kate in her kitchen on the Isle of Palms, South Carolina

Kate Towill

Isle of Palms, South Carolina

It's no surprise that Kate Towill understands hospitality and making friends, family, and visitors feel comfortable. After all, she's spent her married life creating spaces that welcome guests, alongside her husband, Ben, via their firm Basic Projects, including thoughtful spots like the Basic Kitchen, the Post House, and Sullivan's Fish Camp in South Carolina. There is an innate friendliness in these places; they are cool, but not cold, and full of artifacts and serene colors and finishes that mix new and old in the most charming ways. Kate's family house on the Isle of Palms in South Carolina pays all of these ideas forward, too.

After ten years in New York and a move south to Charleston to start Basic Projects, Kate and Ben found their current house at the beach, a ranch that leaned more modern surf shack than their previous old-world abode downtown. "Our vision focused on comfort and durability when it came to the style," Kate says. "When you live at the beach, sandy feet, wet dogs, and children in wet bathing suits inevitably trample in. I didn't want anything to feel too precious, so I used a lot of natural, strong materials, and was very careful not to clutter or overdesign."

Inside, the couple worked with the architect Heather Wilson to open up the space to a garden in the back, focusing first on the areas where the couple hoped to spend the most time. "It's really the center of the house, especially on nice days when you can have the sliding doors off the kitchen fully open and the kids playing soccer in the garden while we drink coffee on the steps," she says.

They also added a guest cottage, which they dubbed the "Love Shack," fittingly. "It was done in a slight panic when I became pregnant again and we were going to lose our guest room," Kate remembers. "We took a long look

This page and opposite: The bedroom and bathroom of the "Love Shack" guesthouse

OCEAN AVENUE

Opposite: The dining room at Kate's house opens to the back garden.

This page: A bevy of blankets and framed memories make for a snug corner.

at our garage and realized we only really needed half of it. We split it with a wall, used a bunch of leftover materials from past projects, and added a bathroom, a tub, and a bed." The result is a sunny, serene spot for their friends to relax after a day at the beach. These days, the couple's two children, hosts in training, draw up handmade welcome notes for visitors.

Kate owes many of her instincts to her education as a set designer (she's a Wes Anderson alum, no less) and to her mom, who encouraged her love of intriguing details, too. "Mom would always mix big antiques with clean millwork," Kate says. "I can remember the hardware latch on a special piece in our kitchen—opening it every day for our plates and glassware. I loved having that connection with something old." So much so that the first thing she purchased for her current kitchen (even before lumber for the renovation) was a display piece similar to the example from her childhood. She even had a wall built to the exact specifications so that it would fit perfectly. "It makes the space," she says.

Perhaps most endearing of all, though, are the handwritten notes at the bottom of framed family photos throughout the house, penned by Ben. "I love for photos to live off our phones and in frames," she says. "And Ben loves the handwritten element on them, too, as a reminder of that moment in time." At the front door, a riot of color on a five-by-eight-foot canvas by

Douglas Diaz greets visitors. "My friend Alexander, who was an auctioneer for Christie's for a long time, told me about Diaz, an abstract artist from Brooklyn now in Bangkok," Kate says. "I sent him a few of my favorite paint colors and he created a custom piece for the house."

And all around, there is lamplight. "With a ranch there are typical low ceilings, so it was important not to fill the house with overhead can lights, which makes it feel like the ceiling is coming down on you," Kate says. "Lamps create a much sexier feeling, with the warm glow of light at your level."

It's the sort of approachable house that makes you want to sit and stay awhile, which visitors to the Towills' no doubt will continue to do for years to come. ■

OLD GOOD THINGS

Seek out pieces that make you think
of comforting memories. For Kate,
it's that weathered sideboard where
she keeps her everyday glassware
and dishes. It's a reminder of a
similar piece from her childhood.

*Heather truly
believes in every
single product she
dreams up and
uses the designs
throughout her house
in Los Angeles.*

THE STORY BEHIND THE STUFF

Linens, Pillows, *and* Bedding

by Heather Taylor of Heather Taylor Home, Los Angeles, California

I feel strongly that it's possible to develop an emotional connection with a material thing. Does it double for priceless human relationships? Of course not, but in the hands of talented designers like Heather Taylor of Heather Taylor Home, the most interesting goods produce big feelings. For me, Heather's table linens and bedding and pillows conjure a sense of peacefulness and relaxation and caring for oneself well. Even perusing photos of her things (triple the effect when actually touching them) makes me feel more okay about the world. These are all ideas that Heather has known intimately since she was a child. "I grew up in a home that valued coziness," she says. "There were lots of classic florals and plaids around our house, and I remember loving my bedroom and taking such joy in decorating my space."

That natural joie de vivre carried into the way Heather entertained as an adult.

"I think it's just an attitude," Heather says. "I genuinely want people to feel relaxed and not worry if they spill something. Along with all the menu planning and cooking, I take such pride in setting the table," she says. Early on in her dinner party endeavors, though, finding the right linens proved difficult. Nothing felt quite like what Heather was hoping for until she found herself in a Saturday-morning weaving class. "When I learned the mechanics and artistry of creating fabric by hand, I realized how much I loved designing fabric and thought I could create my own."

And in 2013 she did just that. Working with artisans in Chiapas, Mexico, who use a weaving technique handed down through generations, Heather dreams up colors and patterns for her table linens, pillows, and bedding. "It usually starts with a color palette inspired by the season," Heather says. "Once we have the

Heather's bedroom features layer upon layer of textiles from her collection.

3.

Authenticity

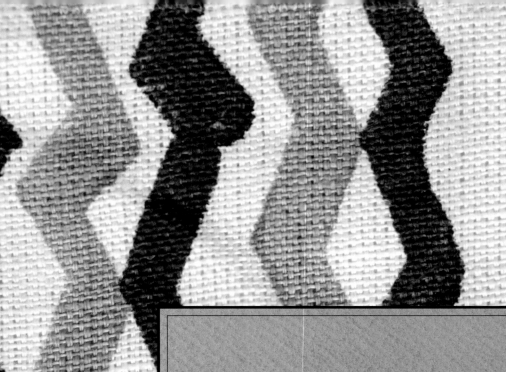

At Home
with
Haskell

All houses have wisdom to impart. Old houses certainly, but new ones, too. In the house of my childhood, the Georgian architecture was as formal as a starched dinner napkin but in need of serious restoration. There was the languid staircase, for starters, and the library and parlor and diamond-lattice windows, a veranda, and even an odd little glass garden conservatory-cum–root cellar for overwintering things from what was once an orchard in the back garden. My parents listened carefully, removing the jumbled evidence that the top two floors served as a dormitory for a decade. They enlisted my mom's siblings and mother and even her grandmother to peel wallpaper from every surface, including the ceilings. Down came the awkward partitionings, and slowly the original grandeur returned. By the time I came along, the house was again a ravishing beauty. The farmhouse that my dad later built by hand for my mom started out as an abandoned tobacco barn in moonshine country, Patrick County, Virginia, in the Blue Ridge Mountains. He listened to that humble history and designed a structure that paid homage to the original, using the same local creek stone and wood construction so that the two talked to one another, a fusion of like minds.

On Grove Street, I was careful to respect the integrity of the architecture of the kitchen. Tall cabinets concealing a pantry and laundry, a painted central island, and playing off the existing tile, floors, windows, and hardware kept everything in harmony.

In my own experience, I did not stumble on such fine specimens. I knew better than to try to make them into something they weren't. In Alabama, I kept all the finishes purposeful and utilitarian, and it suited the place. The same thing happened on Grove Street in Charleston, though I think I listened even harder. I discovered that the original fireplace surround was subway tile from the late thirties, so I used the exact same size and style in the kitchen renovation—not because subway tile is the most glamorous or original idea in the design world but because the house spoke up about it. The same thing happened when I noticed original beadboard ceilings in two other areas. I knew that using the same material again in our bathroom renovation would help make the bathroom fit in, as if it had always been there. I even had a carpenter match the craftsman window and door trim to what was in the original portion of the house to continue that thought.

My favorite architectural addition to Grove Street, though, was the claw-foot tub my dad pulled out of an old house set for demolition and kept in storage for thirty years before it found a home. It communicated instant history, and bathing my baby son in it was such a full-circle moment of generational house love happening in real time. I guess I consider certain details authentic because they are true to the original intent of something and the place where they sit and are

crafted with materials that last: real millwork, real stone, real tile. Nothing plastic, nothing engineered, nothing fake, nothing hollow.

In this chapter, we visit the decorative painter Amy FitzGeorge-Balfour inside her fifteenth-century Tudor house on the southern coast of England in East Sussex. Amy's attention to period detail while also infusing the space with color and whimsy is a remarkable testament to true authenticity. Then we return Stateside to tour the upstate New York retreat by the iconic interior designer Sheila Bridges, a new construction project with roots in the vernacular architecture of the region around it. Next we move on to a traditional house reimagined by the interior designer Georgia Tapert Howe, built in the twenties, old by Los Angeles standards. Finally, we return to the East Coast to view the collections of the antique quilt dealer Jennifer Rho in Richmond, Virginia, to learn more about these incredible examples of genuineness. ◼

I looked to the older utility spaces at Grove Street when designing this bathroom addition, right down to using the same tile, millwork, fixtures, and even bringing more age to the space with a vintage tub. My Dad ripped it out of a derelict house forty years ago and kept it in storage until it landed in its new home.

STYLE WITH SUBSTANCE

Authenticity is an idealistic notion, and old houses—even with all their lovely details—have drawbacks. And while new construction has its perks, investing in genuine details that give a brand-new house patina is most often a luxury of the few. So, if you find yourself facing some of these common issues, here are tweaks that lend a bit more architectural heft.

Hollow-Core Doors

To give them more architectural emphasis than they might otherwise have, switch out the hardware for something heavy and paint them a darker color that jibes with the feel of the house.

Damaged or Nondescript Wood Floors

When in doubt, painting floors adds an enormous amount of charm and helps unite the overall aesthetic of an older home with banged-up floors without the expense of replacing or refinishing them. Painted floors also contribute a layer of interest to ho-hum floors in new construction projects, especially since the technique is typically seen in older houses.

Modern Windows

One way to conceal the lack of dimension of some contemporary windows is in the art of the window treatment. The extra layer of a bamboo blind and drapery panels or a Roman shade can work miracles.

In the hall bath at Grove Street, I loved all the original fixtures, so I barely touched anything, with the exception of adding an extra tall curtain to lift the eye and painting everything (even the ceiling) matte black.

This niche was originally intended for an iron. I turned it into a spice cabinet by simply adding a glass-front door and tiny shelves.

"I CONSIDER CERTAIN DETAILS *AUTHENTIC* BECAUSE THEY ARE TRUE TO THE ORIGINAL INTENT OF SOMETHING AND THE PLACE WHERE THEY SIT AND ARE CRAFTED WITH MATERIALS THAT LAST."

Amy standing outside of her fifteenth-century gem of a house in East Sussex

Amy FitzGeorge-Balfour

Fletching, England

I grew up in Virginia, where the culture, architecture, and interior design are often closely linked to England, so much so that many of the inhabitants have a specific lilt that leans British (just ask someone from Richmond, Virginia, to say *tomato* and you'll understand what I mean), but my love of English design hit me later in life. I did not appreciate the acres of floral chintz fabrics and European antiques and nods to English country houses all around me growing up. I gravitated toward a simpler, cleaner aesthetic. It really wasn't until a few years ago when I observed a newer, more youthful take on the English look that my opinion began to shift. I was influenced by the personality-driven, jubilant work of young tastemakers on the rise, like Matilda Goad, Beata Heuman, and Louise Roe. The spaces they create are feminine and happy and nod ever so faintly to the Bloomsbury Group and their eccen-

tric offerings to the design ethos. There is a decidedly romantic bent to the whole look, and I simply can't get enough of it.

So imagine my delight when I learned about another young English tastemaker, the decorative painter Amy FitzGeorge-Balfour, embellishing mirrors for Wicklewood in London, one of my favorite shops (more on page 267), and began following her house adventure.

At the specific moment I found her, Amy was pregnant with triplets and renovating a Tudor in East Sussex. She and her husband had discovered the property only a few months before. "It's the oldest house in the village with incredible history," Amy says of the circa-fifteenth-century Wealden hall house, which once served as the gatekeeper's cottage and lodge to a sprawling estate nearby. The couple had their work cut out for them. The house was Grade II listed, which is similar to being on the National Register

The library forms a bridge to and from formal and informal rooms in Amy's house.

of Historic Places in the United States, meaning it possessed enough architectural significance to warrant preservation. There was no running water, the electrical was rudimentary and strung via wires between rooms, and there was ample rotting timber and lots of peeling wallpaper. "But it was so charming and begging to be loved back into a family home," Amy says.

And the house was certainly in the right hands. Amy grew up in a family with a creative streak, went on to study illustration in London, and later worked

for Colefax and Fowler, one of the most iconic interior design firms in modern English history. There, she learned under the tutelage of Janie Money, before beginning work on her first house and starting a family. That's when the mood to paint struck. "While I was pregnant, my mother and I took a course with the decorative painter Melissa White at Charleston Farmhouse, and I left hugely inspired, and from that moment on I wanted to paint anything I could get my hands on," she remembers, laughing. Images of her work made their way to

The combination of Amy's hand-painted mantel and lamp and the textiles in the room are illustrative of how she lightened her home's architecture.

A TOUCH OF
THE HAND

Whether you live the storybook
English life or not, items that have
handmade details lend character
and authenticity to a house.
Amy's hand-painted furniture
and other embellishments are a
gobsmackingly beautiful example of
this idea. And even starting small—
with, say, a collection of handmade
wooden spoons in the kitchen—
brings the same idea home.

The kitchen in Amy's house feels simpatico with the age of the house, thanks to a purposeful aesthetic that speaks to both the past and an energetic modern family.

"When it came to choosing finishes, it was important to me that we did not go too modern, or too slavishly traditional, which could have risked coming across as twee."

Instagram, and Amy began getting all sorts of commissions. "I find painting hugely satisfying," she says. "It really is a wonderful way to switch off. Nothing gives me more pleasure than taking these snippets and applying them to a surface with paint."

Amy brought her talent into many corners of her current house. But before those final layers began, she worked alongside an architect to maintain the original elements of the house, while also adding much needed modern systems. The beauty is that it all looks as if it were constructed long, long ago. And that's thanks to Amy's careful eye for authenticity. "When it came to choosing finishes, it was important to me that we did not go too modern, or too slavishly traditional, which could have risked coming across as twee."

To help bring her vision to life, she drew furniture plans and created intricate mood boards. "I wanted to be bold with color and chose to use color on the millwork of the house mostly, rather than the walls, to emphasize the architecture," she says. She also chose a good bit of vintage lighting and plumbing to bring the right sheen of character to things.

In the kitchen and laundry, Amy splurged on in-frame cabinets and installed pine flooring over the existing concrete. "It felt bright, and I knew I didn't want to use tiles or even limestone, as I did not feel it would have been there originally."

Color, often in the form of her decorative embellishments, also lightened the disposition of the Tudor interior. "The house is quite dark, and I was conscious of that," she says. Using bolder colors on the millwork and mixing old and new textiles added the right amount of cheer. "Where there may be a darker corner," she says, "interesting, strong color on a chair or sofa stops a space from feeling gloomy." On mantels and even doorways, Amy's art pulls it all together. "My hand-painted details are an expression of the things that bring me joy, and I think they contribute something completely unique."

And smack in the middle of Amy reimagining her new family home, she gave birth, changing her family of three to a family of six. With her newborns in tow, she continued work, even stenciling the guest bedroom upstairs while the tiny new trio napped on the bed as she applied paint. That tireless effort paid off, and these days you'll find all four children playing tag downstairs. "I think they enjoy the house *very* much," she says.

At the end of my time with Amy, she served soup made from vegetables grown in her extraordinary garden. She is kind, soft-spoken, and quick to laugh. As a fellow young mother, I wished she was just down the street and not across the Atlantic. For now, I'll just have to continue to observe her many projects from afar, and I cannot wait to see what she does next. ∎

Opposite: Amy favors bright rugs layered over seagrass, which brings a fresh look to the historic house.

No truly British house would be complete without a room devoted entirely to a soaking tub, as evidenced by Amy's primary bath.

Amy often changes out the bedding in the primary bedroom and prefers antique American quilts.

Sheila at home in
New York

Sheila Bridges

Livingston, New York

There are some A-list American designers who are talented, to be sure, but remarkably one-note. That is not the case with Sheila Bridges, one of my design heroes. I've followed her closely, as she's not only created memorable homes for clients but also in her personal sphere, from her much-ballyhooed apartment in Harlem to her retreats in Iceland and the Hudson Valley in upstate New York.

I was most intrigued to see, firsthand, Sheila's current escape from the city, an example of new construction, precisely because it is the opposite of the historic home she lived in previously in the area, and of her other homes for that matter. To me, it's illustrative of her range as a designer and an intimate example of how to create something compelling that simultaneously references the place where it sits. "I loved living in an 1880 Colonial with a big porch overlooking

the Hudson River before," she says. "I was surrounded by beautiful land, and my horses, sheep, dogs, goats, and chickens. But my new home has far less maintenance, and it was fun to design something more modern and efficient."

Sheila imagined a barn-inspired structure that fits in neatly with the surrounding farmhouses in the picturesque, bucolic community of Livingston. Inside, the soaring height and white walls of the main living area create a gallery-style backdrop for her astonishing collection of work by change-making Black artists, like Jean-Michel Basquiat, and recent acquisitions from Fabiola Jean-Louis and Kyle Meyer. "My house upstate is much more contemporary than my other homes in Harlem and Reykjavík," she says. "I think one of the most important things was that I created enough wall space to accommodate my love of art. As a designer, I believe that it

This page: The open
shelving at right
in Sheila's kitchen
holds both antique
Wedgewood pieces
and designs from
her collection for
the company.

Opposite: For every
new element in
Sheila's house, there
are older pieces
in equal measure,
like this exceptional
Morroccan rug in the
dining room.

In the dining room, high ceilings echo the barn structures in the agrarian area where Sheila's newly constructed property sits.

"I loved living in an 1880 Colonial with a big porch overlooking the Hudson River before," she says. "I was surrounded by beautiful land, and my horses, sheep, dogs, goats, and chickens. But my new home has far less maintenance, and it was fun to design something more modern and efficient."

is important to be surrounded by things that make you happy and for me, that's art on every wall."

In the middle of all of that boldness, Sheila anchored the space with a collection tied to the land around the house: her bird sculptures. Dozens of the painted wood creatures sit under glass cloches like a Victorian natural history installation. "I have always loved animals and nature in general," she says. "It's where so much of my inspiration comes from. And my friends call my backyard Birdland because there are so many nests. The birds are hand-carved in wood and painted by different artists and artisans, and I'm always looking out for new species." Focus on window ledges and other surfaces here and there, and you'll likely find an actual bird's nest that fell from a nearby tree, only to be rescued and revered indoors.

Sheila's art and collections illustrate the design value of personality, and she continued that notion throughout the rest of the house with her hallmark use of color and pattern. For example, she was careful to design a kitchen that felt at home in a rustic, agrarian-inspired space, while also bringing in saturated, sophisticated color with egg-yolk-yellow cabinetry and a stove to match. To lend a bit of interest in the bedrooms and bathrooms, Sheila combined things like

quilts and historic reproduction wallpaper and hand-painted stripes.

After falling in love with the Hudson Valley decades ago and sheltering in her new space during the pandemic, Sheila, like many creatives transfixed by the region for over a century, isn't going anywhere anytime soon. "Late in the day is probably my favorite time here," Sheila says, looking out over her vegetable garden and the rolling, grassy lawn. "It's when you see the quality of light that inspired painters Frederic Edwin Church and Thomas Cole to come here." ■

Opposite: Sheila's guest bathroom is true to her penchant for stripes (and color), and the millwork, tile, art, and ceiling fixture give it a depth that new construction sometimes lacks.

HISTORY LESSON

Adding antique reproduction
wallpaper to a new construction
house lends history. Bridges did
an impeccable job of this in her
guest bedroom at her Hudson
house by installing an eighteenth-
century geometric motif from
the archives at Adelphi Paper
Hangings (see page 266).

A very small selection of Sheila's extensive bird collection inside her New York house

Georgia in the entryway of her house in Los Angeles. The art is by Marian McEvoy.

Georgia Tapert Howe

Los Angeles, California

Sometimes kismet leads the way. That's certainly what ushered me to Georgia Tapert Howe and her 1920s-style home in the oldest neighborhood in Los Angeles. Georgia and her husband are New York natives transplanted in the land of the lotus eaters. And she also happens to be the other half of Brier & Byrd, the wallpaper company she founded alongside the Charleston artist Lia Burke Libaire, whom you'll meet in the next chapter (see page 243). Lia settled in Charleston after years spent in both New York and Los Angeles, and she suggested I would enjoy meeting Georgia. Lia was correct in that assumption.

When I stepped over the threshold, it just so happened to be during one of the worst flooding events in California history. Unseasonably cold, with drenching rain pouring down outside and forming currents of water in the street. And yet inside, all was aglow.

"I often think when I go into a great house," says Georgia, "'Oh, this is a dinner-party house,' meaning I want to spend time with friends there." And that's the exact feeling she cultivated throughout her family's space. It feels like part intellectual salon and part family house, set against the backdrop of Georgian architecture. "I loved that it was an old house that had almost all of the original details," Georgia says. "I walked in and could instantly imagine us there. I used to walk past it and always wondered what the house was like inside because it didn't look like other houses in the area." In other words, the space had an innate authenticity, and Georgia is a house romantic.

She kept nearly all the original floors, windows, crown molding, mantels, paneling, and generally anything with a wallop of old-house élan. "A lot of people want to get rid of those details, but for us, it's

GETTING THE BONES RIGHT

One area of the original house that Georgia did decide to change was the linoleum floor in the kitchen. She swapped it out for something that might have been used in a Georgian house in its heyday, selecting marble checkerboard tiles that will only get better as the years go by.

Georgia paid close attention to the original finishes in the house when designing the kitchen, and added a family photo collection above the breakfast nook.

Georgia's dining room features molding endemic to the Georgian architecture of the house.

"I loved that it was an old house that had almost all of the original details. I walked in and could instantly imagine us there."

what we loved." She also brought a bit of the East Coast along, in the form of a few heirloom furniture pieces she had growing up, and peppered every room with distinctive details, from the wall of family snapshots in the breakfast room to her portrait by Enoc Perez downstairs and the renderings of her children by Alexander Newley on the upstairs landing.

Also upstairs, Georgia installed the most popular print in her wallpaper line with Lia, a giant blue-and-white repeat of artichokes on the vine. The overscale, happy motif is transportive in an *Alice in Wonderland* sort of way and anchors the spot where her children play.

The whole family spent a lot of time in all the rooms during the pandemic. "I was so grateful that we got to be in this house through it all," she says. Still, Georgia, who honed her skills working for David Easton and Mica Ertegun before founding her own firm, opening a retail shop in New York, and moving west, never pictured herself staying in California. "We kept thinking we would go back to New York City," she says of the move thirteen years ago. "But we couldn't quite tear ourselves away from the easy lifestyle and the space. And now it really feels like home." ■

Opposite: The vernacular windows in the house remain in the playroom upstairs that Georgia papered in "Artichoke Vine," by Brier & Byrd.

This page: Georgia framed a collection of illustrations from the book Pre-Pop Warhol, *by Jesse Kornbluth, to delineate an area for work off the living room.*

THE STORY BEHIND THE STUFF

Antique Quilts

from Jennifer Rho of Flying Geese, Richmond, Virginia

Antique quilts, like all things of a certain age and provenance, are on a short list of authentic items for the home. And as is the case with all circular design trends, their historic patterns reentered the limelight in interiors and in fashion recently. But at their very essence, antique quilts and really all textiles of a certain ilk defy "in" and "out" labels. Stretching back through the eons, nearly every culture repurposed tired textiles into some other useful form. American antique quilts are familiar emblems of resourcefulness, creativity, and resilience.

For an antique quilt whose beauty matches the research and love that went into saving it, Jennifer Rho of Flying Geese is a curator to know. Her business, based in Richmond, Virginia, began as a joining of the minds with a friend and domestic abuse survivor who wanted to shine light on this female-driven craft. "Celebrating quilts—a form of textile art that has been predominantly created by women and not coincidentally under-valued—seemed like the perfect vehicle to highlight the invisible work of women's hands past and present, while also providing a way to raise money for organizations that actively help women in need," Jennifer says. When her cofounder went in a different direction, she continued the noble work benefiting charities like the House of Ruth and the Tahirih Justice Center.

Most of Jennifer's quilt offerings, coordinated by color or style, are sold through Instagram. Like any piece of art, no two are exactly alike. Ever. "Even two quilts created in the same pattern and colorway will be different because of the quilter's level of skill, choice of quilting pattern, and their personal touch," she says. Her favorites include feedsack quilts from the thirties and forties. "With the commercialization of the sewing machine, a wide range of beautiful print fabrics were created to package and promote grains and sugars, which women then saved and used to make clothing and quilts. Born of a time of frugality, they are a distinct representation of a specific historical era when women used what they had to create objects of necessity, but also of beauty. It's particularly exciting to find little remnants of prints from advertising on feedsacks, often on the back of some of these quilts."

The real rarity is tracking provenance. "So many quilts have been passed down or sent to thrift stores or auction houses without any trace of the maker," Jennifer says. "So when you find a small note, pinned or stitched to a quilt with family information, that is truly exciting." Size, though, is a general clue into the history. "Quilts were generally larger before the 1890s. In the following decades, quilts are more of what we would consider a full size today," she says. "People who are new to quilts will sometimes ask about a king-sized quilt. Those did not really come into existence until after king-sized beds came on the market in the fifties and sixties.

"The most touching stories are ones where a family member recounts memories that are tied up with a specific quilt, often ones of a grandmother or mother, who love them with the work of their hands." Reviving each piece to sell after years in storage or bouncing around antiques stores is a painstaking endeavor. "My laundering process is guided by my assessment on the condition and fragility of a quilt and my end goal. For quilts that will likely be very undesirable without the removal of some significant staining, I will take the risk of soaking in a stain-removing detergent, anywhere from minutes to several hours," Jennifer says. "Others just need a freshening and soak, and for those I will use anything from eco-friendly, gentle clothing detergent to Eucalan to a squirt or two of dish liquid. I have washed many quilts that have not been laundered for over a century, and though they may appear to be relatively clean, you realize upon washing that they are indeed very dirty. They often require at least three or four or more rinses in the tub. The drying process requires draining the water, and then carefully lifting the quilt onto a rack and allowing it to drip for a while. Then I move the quilt gently to a large towel or two and let it drip dry on there to release the quilt of some of the water weight. During the winter, I will then drape the quilt over one of my banisters, and in the summer outside. Shifting the quilt around during the drying process, especially in the first hour, is important, as it may stretch in the spots where it's being hung."

Research and washing and folding aside, Jennifer maintains that the best way of all to show appreciation for her pieces is "to use and enjoy!" ■

Clockwise from top left:

Jennifer at home; a Double Irish Chain quilt, c. 1900; washing a calico quilt by hand; a Log Cabin quilt, c. 1880

A star pattern quilt sourced c. 1880, found in Berks County, Pennsylvania

"When you find a small note, pinned or stitched to a quilt with family information, that is truly exciting."

4.

FLAIR

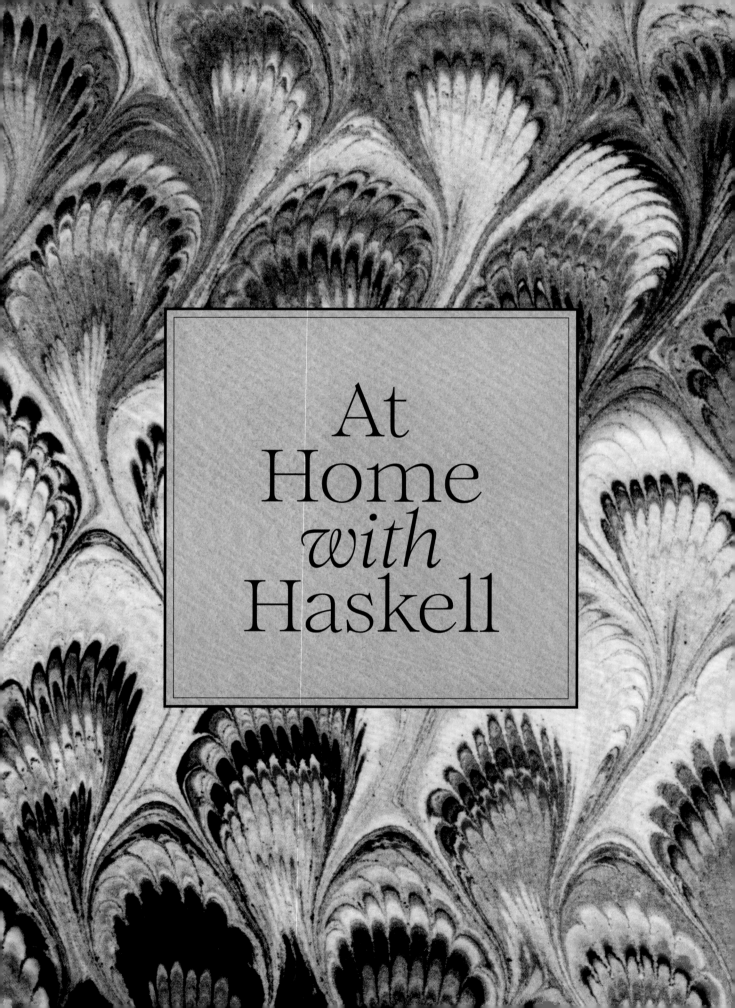

At Home with Haskell

I used to wonder all the time as a child, and especially as a teenager, how stylish people became stylish. Were they born with it? Was it learned? Where did one go and what did one study in order to become "stylish"? The answer, as I came to find out one step at a time, is having an interest in it to begin with and paying attention to the world: the people, the houses, the clothes, the food, the art, the gardens, the objects, and the beauty in it. Getting lost in reading books about it, traveling to places known for it, soaking up takeaway ideas from magazine images, always looking up (that ceiling color!) and looking down (that tile!), and behaving all the while like a sponge. With the lovely accumulation of all this knowledge, we find out what we like, what we gravitate toward, what moves us and makes a little buzzing, humming sensation enter our minds. We start to know when some aesthetic thing (a shade of lipstick, an overflowing library, a very odd but bewitching table lamp) announces who we are without saying a word. That's how signature style develops—out of that education of watching and observing and sometimes tweaking classical ideas to make them your very own.

Pattern and color have always been a passion for me. I felt that whirring, glowing feeling when I saw Pucci and Liberty of London fabrics for the first time. I spent hours as a child turning the pages of my mom's wallpaper sample books in her interior design offices, admiring each one slowly and tracing the names with my finger on the covers: Scalamandré, Schumacher, Osborne & Little, Cowtan & Tout, Brunschwig & Fils, and on and on.

For me, pattern is an art that can be enjoyed on a human, everyday scale. When I was a young editor, my passion turned to paper arts of all kinds. I started collecting wrapping paper, marbled paper, paper flowers, and papier-mâché pieces. Gradually, I also taught myself how to decoupage things with paper, and the thought occurred to me that decoupage was similar to wallpaper and I could likely do it on walls. I'd seen a few examples in books before, too, so I had a hunch it would work. On Grove Street, I decoupaged a hallway that got very little natural light with marbled paper. I wanted it to look a bit like broken blue-and-white china, so I tore the paper into pieces and covered not only the walls but the ceiling, too. Because of the movement in the pattern, the finished space felt taller, bigger, and way more interesting.

And it added something a bit different to the mix that I knew I wouldn't see anywhere else. I didn't purchase it somewhere; I dreamed it up myself. And there is real satisfaction in knowing yourself and what you love well enough to charge forward with confidence. To me, that is the very essence of flair and personal style. One note of caution is that at some point restraint is necessary. I knew when to say when with the decoupage. Otherwise, we would have soon been living in a piñata. But believing in your version of what thoughtful, singular style can be? Do that with abandon.

In this chapter, we visit two Texas style mavens: first, the tastemaker Natalie Steen, whose home in Houston shows that art is definitely her love language; then, the inimitable mix master Kim West in her patterned jewel box of a house in Austin. Both women have a firm understanding of what they love and how to bring those interests to life in their homes. To wrap things up, we sit down in the studio with the collage artist Isabel Bornstein, who creates the sort of intimate portraits of family members that are intended to stay with their owners for generations and add meaning to their walls. That sort of flair makes them all worthy house romantics. ■

Opposite: I papered the hallway in the Grove Street house with marbled paper table runners from Hester & Cook. I tore rolls of it to make the finished product look a bit like broken heirloom china.

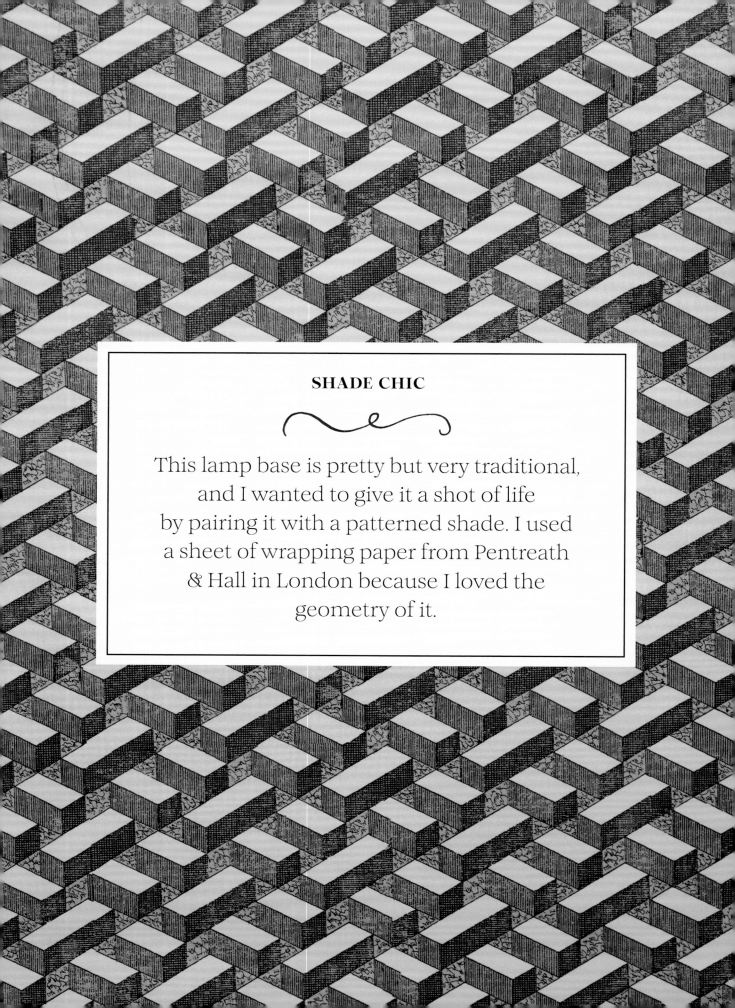

SHADE CHIC

This lamp base is pretty but very traditional,
and I wanted to give it a shot of life
by pairing it with a patterned shade. I used
a sheet of wrapping paper from Pentreath
& Hall in London because I loved the
geometry of it.

Opposite: "Tortoise" wrapping paper, by Caspari

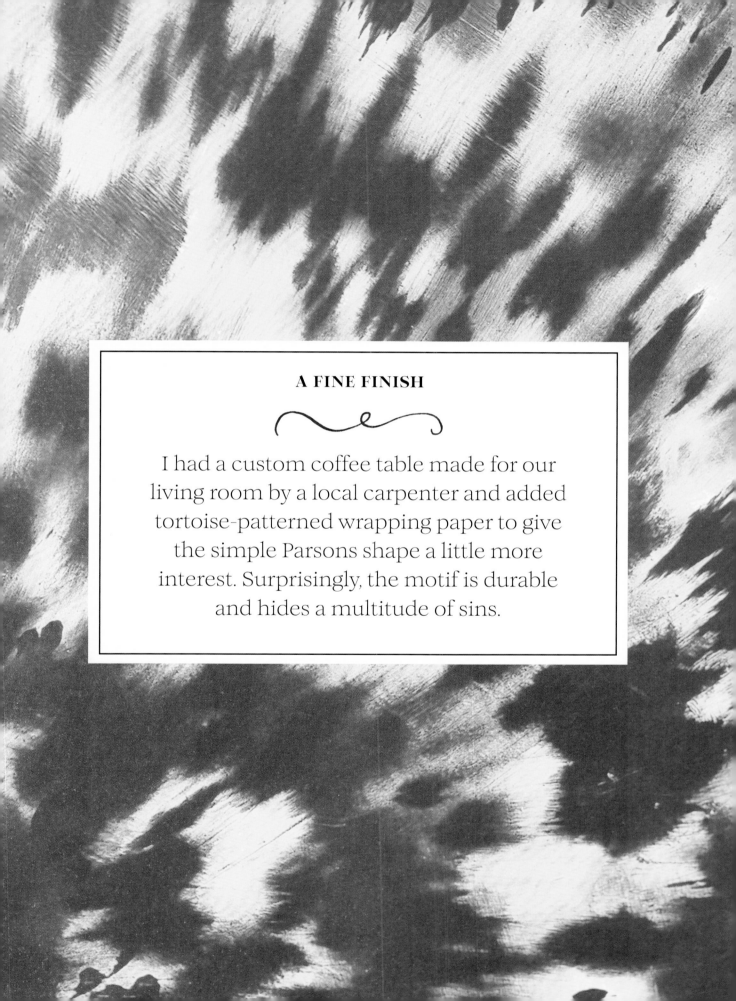

A FINE FINISH

I had a custom coffee table made for our living room by a local carpenter and added tortoise-patterned wrapping paper to give the simple Parsons shape a little more interest. Surprisingly, the motif is durable and hides a multitude of sins.

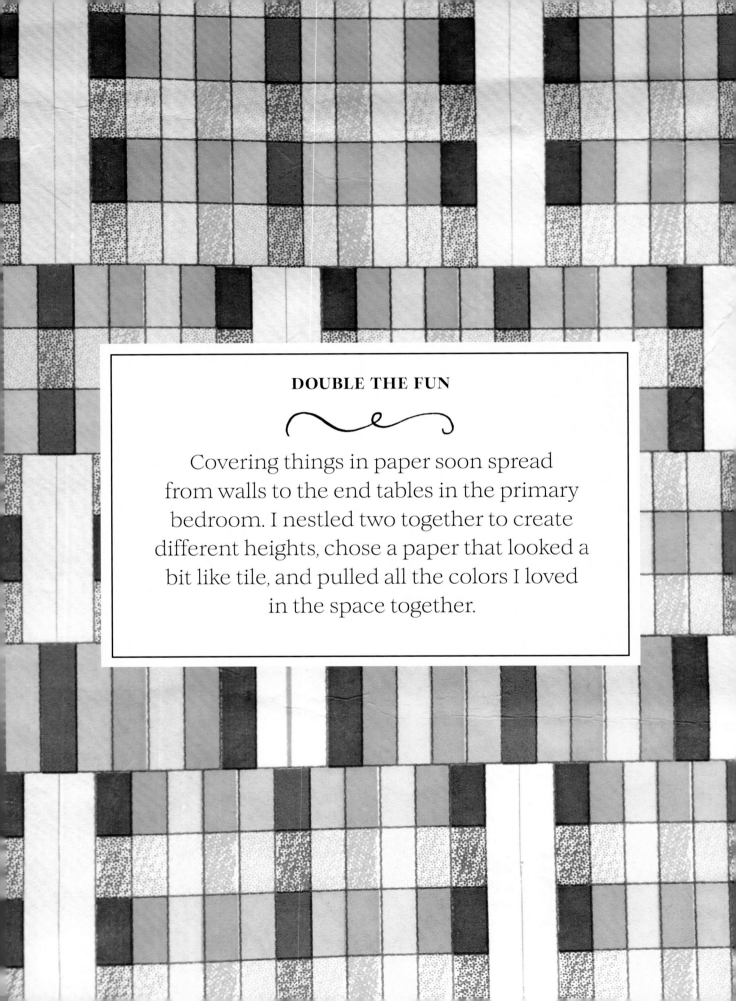

DOUBLE THE FUN

Covering things in paper soon spread
from walls to the end tables in the primary
bedroom. I nestled two together to create
different heights, chose a paper that looked a
bit like tile, and pulled all the colors I loved
in the space together.

Opposite: Fine art paper with a geometric motif

I papered my dressing room in the Grove Street house with botanical book pages from *Florilegium, by Basilius Besler,* to bring a bit of the garden inside. And my vanity chair has been painted no less than seventy-five times; I never tire of the shape or switching hues.

"THERE IS REAL
SATISFACTION
IN KNOWING
YOURSELF AND
WHAT YOU LOVE
WELL ENOUGH
TO CHARGE
FORWARD WITH
CONFIDENCE."

Natalie at home in Houston. The lacquer she used on the walls involved many, many, many coats of Benjamin Moore Milkshake.

Natalie Steen

Houston, Texas

In the last decade, the way human beings shop for goods has profoundly shifted in the direction of influencers and social media. So much so that I personally find it hard to entirely connect with and sift through the massive onslaught most days. Even having spent most of my adult life as a market and style editor, I find it overwhelming and am constantly on the lookout for something different and more engaging. I've admired the format Natalie Steen provides in her weekly newsletter, *The Nat Note*, from the beginning. For starters, it arrives once a week, not five times a day—which means her communication feels special and I look forward to it—and because Natalie, who is based in Houston, Texas, skips all the fluff and gets right to it. We are also in a similar chapter of life, working motherhood, and she has a dynamite eye for interesting things, be they small-batch children's clothes or handmade glassware. When I

first had the pleasure of getting to know her a bit better, I learned that in addition to her burgeoning social media role, she's also a whip-smart former lawyer and a second-generation Cuban American with an incredibly quick wit.

Her house, as you might imagine, embodies this swirling diversity. It's fun, but studied, too, and the art immediately jumps out. One such piece is a very modern portrait of Steen's grandmother by an artist collective in Lebanon called Sarah's Bag, created using a vintage photograph. Steen's grandmother escaped from Cuba during the revolution, along with the rest of Steen's family, with only the clothes on their backs. "They left the beautiful island they called home, and with it, everything they had ever owned," Natalie says. Without heirlooms to tell her family story and to draw on for her own personal style, she created her own. "This metaphorical blank slate inspired

A piece by Adelaide Cioni arrests attention in the dining room, as does the abstract by Mitch Lewis in the foreground.

me to fill my closet and my home with things that are meaningful," she says.

"I have my sister-in-law, Illa Gaunt, to thank for my deeper and more informed appreciation of art. She is an art consultant, and under her wing, we have acquired a mix of work that spans different mediums." Some of Steen's favorite pieces include work by Kikuo Saito, Chuck Ramirez, Grace Weaver, Monica Kim Garza, Kelly O'Connor, and Matt Kleberg. Another standout is the giant piece by Adelaide Cioni in the dining room, as well as the abstract by Mitch Lewis, and Natalie also champions emerging artists like Sarabeth Arima, who created a portrait of her oldest son.

The house itself *is* an heirloom of sorts, from her husband's Texan side of the family. "Our merging of styles mimicked our merging of cultures," she says. "It's a little bit cowboy and a little bit Cuban." When it came to color and fabrics, Natalie turned to the designer Lila Malone to home in on her history. "I needed someone to help me make sense of it all," she says. In turn, Lila chose bold hues and patterns. The living room is lacquered pink—one might even say *Cuban* pink. "It resembles the inside of a seashell, and the high-gloss finish makes everyone look their best while triggering a subconscious desire for a cocktail," Natalie says with a laugh. In the dining room and entry, Lila chose Katibi by Brunschwig & Fils and Sameera by Lee

Jofa, wallpapers with tropical inflections. And in Steen's office, inside a glass box on display with her many accolades, is the exact pair of shoes her grandmother was wearing when she escaped all those years ago. The ultimate heirloom. "My family's greatest lesson to me has been to find whatever it is I am passionate about and to excel in it," Natalie says.

Looking around her house in Houston, she succeeded and then some. ∎

In the primary bedroom is a diptych by Layla Luna that Natalie commissioned to symbolize the Texas landscape.

A gem vase by John Torreano anchors the coffee table vignette.

MORE THAN
MEETS
THE EYE

Art is the peak form of flair, and Natalie pulls this idea off in a particularly moving way. For example, because her maternal grandmother barely escaped with her life and the clothes on her body when she fled Cuba during the revolution, Natalie doesn't have the conventional accoutrement passed down through generations that some families do, so her walls do the storytelling. This particular piece, by a team of female artists Natalie discovered on Etsy called Sarah's Bag, uses a vintage photograph of her grandmother as well as textiles to craft an entirely original take on the "family portrait."

A photo from a San Antonio charreada by Minta Maria hangs in the breakfast room.

"OUR MERGING OF
STYLES MIMICKED
OUR MERGING OF
CULTURES. IT'S A
LITTLE BIT COWBOY
AND A LITTLE
BIT CUBAN."

Kim at home
in Austin

Kim West

Austin, Texas

Mixing patterns in interiors with a deft hand is an art form. The genre is infinitely trickier when it comes to combining lots of patterns in one space. But under the guidance of a gifted mix master, the result isn't loud, it's vivacious. Kim West, the owner of Supply Showroom in Austin, Texas, is what I call a pattern-on-pattern savant, not only in her choices for the kicky headquarters of the business she cofounded but especially in her quirky Victorian home just off South Congress Avenue. "Living in a pattern-filled home brings so much joy to our lives," she says. "The world is a crazy place; life is hard, and for us living in a home like this, it feels like a respite."

Kim, who grew up in Texas and London, wound up in fashion in New York, traveling all over the world and absorbing style nuances wherever she went. "Working for Jil Sander added a touch of masculinity in all my design preferences. Then working at Marc Jacobs let me fully unleash an over-the-top, playful aesthetic." Eventually the road led back home to Austin, where she initially worked as an interior designer. "I realized quickly how I loved design but actually didn't want to work with private clients," she remembers. A short time later, Callie Jenschke, a former shelter magazine editor in New York newly arrived in Texas, approached Kim with the idea of opening a showroom. With their mutual friend Kristin Gish, a brand-new business was born. "Austin didn't have many options for design sourcing, and our whole model was representing independent artists who wanted to be in Texas," says Kim. Today that means the trio brings tiny, fashion-forward lines like Annie Coop and Imogen Heath to the rapidly expanding Texas design stage—and sometimes offers their first foray into the American market.

After nine years of coveting her dream house and passing it longingly on walks, it finally came up for sale. Kim and her

In the primary bedroom, Kim enveloped the room in a wallpaper by Abigail Borg. She paired that with additional prints by Isobel on the headboard and bedskirt, and yet another by Lulie Wallace on the sofa.

family moved in, and she began experimenting at home with what she and her team were discovering for clients. "We call it the dollhouse because of the choppy layout and charming rooms," she says. "For a wallpaper fanatic, the floorplan is ideal for pattern overdrive." Kim counts thirteen wallpaper motifs currently, with more no doubt on the way. She started with dusty pink and green in the library, dining room, and kitchen, and sorbet colors in the remaining downstairs areas. "It's like living in candy," she says. Her recipe for combining prints is always the same. "Once I sort out the palette in a space, I start to play with the patterns. I think about scale, which pattern is the star, and which patterns support. My absolute favorite thing is a patterned sofa. They are so much better for kids because spills don't show up quite like they do on a solid."

Upstairs, Kim went full throttle with a single pattern by Australia's Abigail Borg in her primary bedroom on nearly every surface. The effect is almost tentlike thanks to the quirky eaves. It's the perfect perch to watch the sun set on the city—and dream about her next inspiration trip. "Never-ending curiosity and wanderlust are basically my porn. Add a sparkle and a pattern and *shoosh*, I'm done!" ◼

Opposite: The wallpaper in Kim's bar is by Louise Jones.

This page: In the TV room, a floral by Abigail Borg mashes up delightfully with wallpaper by Faye Bell and drapery panels in a print by Maresca Textiles.

The TV room in Kim's Austin house is a study in mix mastery.

"Once I sort out the palette in a space, I start to play with the patterns. I think about scale, which pattern is the star, and which patterns support."

DON'T RUSH IT

It's so easy to stress over doing everything to a house all at once to give it flair. But most of the time, the truly showstopping moments happen over time. Kim dreamed about having a chandelier from the fabled glass artisans in Murano, Italy, from the time she was a little girl, and that made finding the ideal topper for her dining room all the sweeter.

Isabel's portrait of my little boy at age three, eating an ice cream sandwich

Collage Work

by Isabel Bornstein of Borna Collage, Charleston, South Carolina

The artist Isabel Bornstein landed Stateside only a few short years ago, and the moment I first saw her collage work, I was captivated—not just by the use of color in her pieces but also her clever combinations of materials. In person she's unassuming and warm, and her enthusiasm for what she creates is infectious. I was most attracted to her portraits of children. I love old-fashioned ones, too, for capturing a fleeting moment in time, but I wanted a portrait of my little boy that was a bit unusual, not traditional.

To me, portraits are in a category of art that instantly instills the home where they hang with meaning and with a family narrative. Isabel understands this idealistic notion of what they add to a house because she grew up in a place with extraordinary history.

She spent her formative years in Buenos Aires. "My mother is a painter and writer and has always been such a huge supporter of anything creative in my life," she says. "There was never a lack of colored pencils at home." Her father owns a wonderful design shop called 30quarenta, and Isabel first dabbled in collage while working for him as a teenager. "We would go to flea markets, antiques shops, art galleries, and auction houses on weekends," she remembers. "At the time this seemed a little odd, but now I'm thankful to have had that exposure so early."

And it makes sense that she works in the world of collage as an adult, given her own geographical and cultural layerings. Her pieces often combine paper, paint, and photographs, and I was immediately drawn to their depth of field. When she started work on my little boy's portrait, she summed up his plucky personality with a wink. It all started with a photo of him gleefully eating an ice-cream sandwich. Isabel then set his

A table in Isabel's studio overflows with recent work incorporating watercolor and collage of cut figures from Slim Aarons photography books and Audubon tomes.

"I love creating
portraits because
I feel like I get a
glimpse into
what brings other
people joy."

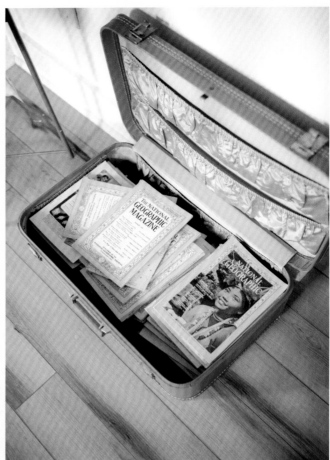

Left to right: Cutting and pasting figures for future collages; a suitcase of vintage
National Geographic *magazines that Isabel often uses in her work*

silhouette against an eighteenth-century architectural rendering of a building in Paris atop a painted halo of stripes. It's now my favorite piece of art. It's all I can do to hold myself back from commissioning a pet portrait of my dog, Auggie (because Isabel does those, too). "I love creating portraits because I feel like I get a glimpse into what brings other people joy," Isabel says.

Lately I'm also drawn to her retro beach and pool culture collages, in which she incorporates watercolor stripes and clever cutouts from books of Slim Aar-

ons's leisure lifers. Her food collages are particularly hilarious as well, like the recent work depicting a seventies surfer from a LeRoy Grannis book gliding down the edge of a hot dog clipped from an old *Gourmet* magazine.

Isabel often rises early to start work, scissors whirring away over the outlines. "I'm not a very patient painter or a good photographer, so by doing collage I get to celebrate artists I admire," she says. "I like the idea of bringing them out of a coffee-table book and onto the wall, in a new context and an imaginary world." ■

Isabel at
home in her
Charleston studio

5.

NATURE

At Home with Haskell

I'm looking at a picture of a little girl and an elderly woman bending to examine a row of flowers. The little girl is me, and the elderly woman is my paternal grandmother. The place is her garden in Kinston, North Carolina. I remember the day because it was the visit where she taught me that snapdragons talk. "If you squeeze them just like this," she said, pinching the hinge on the bloom, "they'll open their little mouths to say hello." And they did. And I was mesmerized. She also taught me, because as a minister's wife she never properly owned a home or piece of land in her life, that it's a noble thing to leave a place better than you found it.

What she really meant by that is: Leave it better by planting a garden. Add something alive and beautiful; add something that will bring spiritual and physical sustenance, even if it is not yours to see to fruition. I believe this, too. As does my dad, who seems to have planted forests of trees over the course of his life. The pine saplings he planted at the farmhouse he built when I was a toddler and where I spent many of my childhood weekends are nearly my age now. And his hollies at my parents' current home in Virginia are old ladies, too, as are the hundreds of peonies I helped my mom plant after we found tubers for sale during a trip to Winterthur, the Dupont estate in Delaware, when I was fifteen. The first flush of peonies is always in late April in my parents' garden, where these blooms blanket an entire hillside in fragrance.

All that exposure to the romance and emotional investment of living with plants followed me long after I left home and held sway even when I didn't have a proper place to dig in the earth. When I first moved to Charleston, for example, and rented an apartment inside a nineteenth-century house on Meeting Street, I found a way to create a solarium of sorts inside. Where there was a sunny spot, there were pots and pots of things leaning into the sun. And no, at that time I didn't have the luxury of cutting flowers to bring inside, but I often tucked blooms in my pockets on my walks around the city and placed them in vases when I got home. And I've always been drawn to botanicals in art form to bring a bit of a garden into every room, be they in the form of a traditional rendering or something more modern like the paper sculptures depicting foxgloves and geraniums from the Green Vase by Livia Cetti. Living with plants, in whatever form that takes, is another critical element of being a house romantic.

It wasn't until the pandemic, however, that I truly grasped the sanctuary a garden provides—even if it's just an escape for a few hours from a house you love.

There is something exhilarating and exhausting about getting dirty, digging, weeding, moving plants, cutting plants back, training plants, and planning, always planning, for the future while admiring the progress of the present. Early in lockdown, my favorite way to start the day with my then toddler was in the garden. He was always up before sunrise, as was I, and as soon as the first bit of light hit the front windows, we bolted out to see what was blooming. Among his first utterances after "Mamu" and "dat dog" were "zinnia" and "rose" and "Monty Don" (he loved watching the beloved British landscape designer on television). Then he helped me water and pointed out butterflies and played for hours until it was time to start the work-from-home-while-also-entertaining-a-child day.

Those early mornings saved me from monotony and worry over the world and many other, deeper stressors. Just hearing birdsong or smelling the salvia and germander and tea olive when I pruned those aromatic plants soothed me. It was in those precious hours that I also brought flowers inside to arrange and place here and there as a symbol of the calm the garden brought me. My son liked to sit at the kitchen island with me to help, sometimes filling empty glass soda bottles with extra blooms for his Montessori teachers. When it rained and we couldn't go outside, I would take him to the win-

For the porch on Grove Street, I used a handful of outdoor fabrics by Sunbrella in blues, peaches, pinks, and reds and repurposed a pair of vintage Brown Jordan chairs. I also had a custom storage bench made and painted the floor with a bright pop of color.

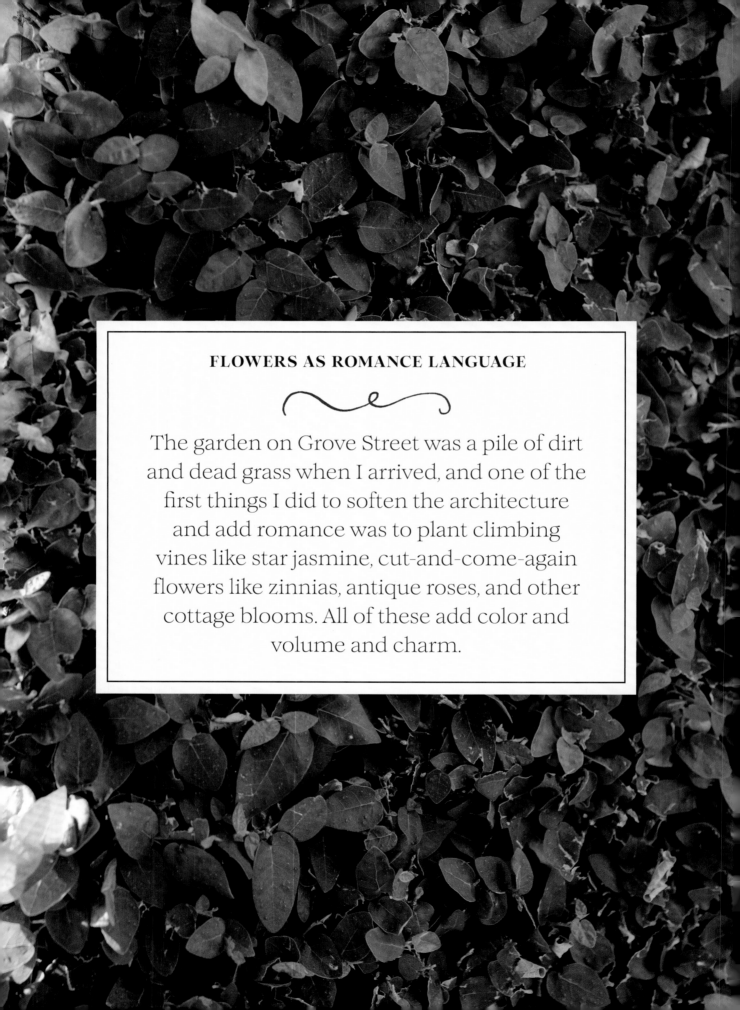

FLOWERS AS ROMANCE LANGUAGE

The garden on Grove Street was a pile of dirt and dead grass when I arrived, and one of the first things I did to soften the architecture and add romance was to plant climbing vines like star jasmine, cut-and-come-again flowers like zinnias, antique roses, and other cottage blooms. All of these add color and volume and charm.

Star jasmine

Belinda's Blush roses

Salvia

Rosemary

A baby zinnia grown from seed from Floret Flowers, one of my favorite sources for seeds

"There is something exhilarating and exhausting about getting dirty, digging, weeding, moving plants, cutting plants back, training plants, and planning, always planning, for the future while admiring the progress of the present."

dows and show him the different flowers "getting a drink of water." For me and for my little boy, it was almost as if there were no line between our house and our garden and that the roses and billowy star jasmine were as much a part of our daily landscape as the dining room table or his crib.

My experience with the garden on Grove Street only deepened my belief that any form of interacting with a flower or a tree or a blade of grass is essential. Even if you can't garden outside, there is always a way to bring the idea of one into your space and reap similar rewards.

In this chapter, we'll travel to meet the artist Susan Hable in Athens, Georgia,

first. Many of Susan's paintings depict flora, and seeing the landscape where her studio sits brings a new understanding of living and working near the natural world. Then it's all the way to New York to see the interior designer Barrie Benson and her summer house, which is the most idyllic example of a space that blurs the line between indoors and out that I've seen. It's a dreamscape sort of place. And then, for gardening by osmosis, we sit with the artist Lia Burke Libaire to learn more about her playful take on the age-old idea of painting traditional subjects like fruits, vegetables, flowers, and leaves and decorating with them indoors. ■

*Opposite, left to right:
Evolvulus Blue Daze, a
dwarf variety of morning
glory that I planted along
the picket fence line; an
electric pink geranium,
an eighties favorite and
one of mine, too*

*This page: Icy blue
lobelia, a tumble-y
stunner*

Susan in front
of her studio

Susan Hable

Athens, Georgia

Susan Hable is hilarious. The kind of funny where you cannot catch your breath. The magnetic kind. I never know each time I visit her what color her hair might be or what inventive combination of jewels and Comme des Garçons and vintage she might be sporting or if her nails might be shellacked with rainbow glitter. I do know my time with her always leaves me moved not only by her talent as an artist but also by her infectious sense of humor (and mischief).

After years of living in New York, Susan moved to Athens, Georgia, and started a garden from scratch for the first time in her adult life. "My mom is an avid gardener, and I did always admire gardens but never thought I would one day have my own to make and take care of," she says. "When we bought the house, it was a blank slate, but once the pandemic came, the garden was starting to mature."

During the pandemic, she found herself as intertwined with her landscape as I did. She's always turned to nature in her work, but it took on another level of meaning when the world turned upside down. "I garden to escape but it also hits my obsessive buttons," she says. "I always tell people that when I can't move my furniture around anymore, I go and move dirt around. I wander there when I'm needing a break or inspiration. My wheels are always turning, and sometimes things just need to marinate to turn into ideas."

It's easy to understand why this place offers such a captivating spot to think: Her current studio sits like a temple in the middle of a rolling expanse of green that leads to the main house. "We live in a Victorian house, so I wanted plants that are an extension of the era of the house," she says. "I've made countless mistakes but over the last eleven years here, it

As you enter Susan's garden from the main house, the vista of her studio at the rear is pure fairy-tale, with overflowing beds flanking the sloping lawn.

Susan clipping and snipping

"I always tell people that when I can't move my furniture around anymore, I go and move dirt around. I wander there when I'm needing a break or inspiration. My wheels are always turning, and sometimes things just need to marinate to turn into ideas."

Pearl bush

Boutonniere rose

Mock orange

Darcey Bussell rose, by David Austin

ANTIQUE FINDS

Susan is no stranger to seeking out wonderful objects from the past for the interior of her house, and the same goes for specimens in her rambling garden. The array of older varieties of plants she's collected gives the entire landscape a grounded, history-rich feeling. Every tender leaf and fragrant blossom has a narrative, from the spray of Peggy Martin roses over her arbor that "people wreck their cars looking at" to the brooch-like blooms of her pearl bushes. Following Susan's example is easy to do in your own garden or on a sunny windowsill; it just takes a bit of imagination and research. For some of my favorite resources for one-of-a-kind plants, see page 267.

Left to right: A sitting area outside Susan's studio; Susan arranging things from garden

seems to be the only way to learn." As you might imagine, there are roses galore and many, many climbing plants, such as Susan's wily, variegated porcelain vine that travels over the surface of the screen porch. "Most of my special things came from a recently closed nursery in Lexington, Kentucky, called Goodness Grows. My dear friend Rick Berry would point me in the direction of any plant that was 'old-timey,' as he knew that was my goal." And the most gratifying part of all of it for Susan was bringing the blooms in. "After getting used to spending so much money on flowers in the flower district in New York, the fact that I cut my own flowers is so incredible."

In the South, the heat is too strong midday to properly work under it or enjoy being outside, and Susan's favorite times are around dawn and dusk. "I like the end of the day to putter. Dusk is hazy in the summer, and the light is dreamy," she says. "But morning is cooler and is the best time to pull thirty minutes of weeds. There is always work in my garden. That job is never done!" ∎

A variegated porcelain vine grows wild and free on Susan's screen porch.

Barrie relaxing on her porch in Chautauqua, a space that spills out into the garden

Barrie Benson

Chautauqua, New York

I've drooled over the work of the Charlotte, North Carolina, interior designer Barrie Benson for as long as I can remember. Each time she shares a new project, what strikes me immediately is her singular point of view. In my opinion, no one else in the design world combines completely diverging ideas and periods of furniture in one house and makes it all sing quite like she does. And while Barrie deeply understands and respects ladylike old-school traditions, she also revels in breaking many of those rules, an irreverent quality that drew me to her projects (and her personality) from the start. I first met Barrie working on a story for *Garden & Gun*, and I'm so lucky to call her my friend twenty-odd years later. She is as generous of spirit in person as the rooms she creates.

And I've always been curious about her summer house. It's a place she seems to disappear into only to reappear each

fall full of renewed energy. It was all very mysterious and intriguing until I finally made the trek (nearly to Canada) to see it in upstate New York. I get it now. Barrie's 1899 kit house is one of dozens of interesting Victorian-era styles of architecture that dot the secretive enclave of Chautauqua, New York, a place where some of America's greatest intellectual minds have been summering with their families for over a hundred years. It's like stepping into a rarified universe where no one is in a hurry. Oh, and it's achingly beautiful.

"The second I arrive, I start sleeping well. It's almost like a reset for my circadian clock," Barrie says. "I cook more, I relax more, I sleep more, and the cool air is blissful. Although I do work, I do it in a limited fashion and have structured my business so I can take this time off in the summer, and I'm very thankful for my team in Charlotte who allow this to

This page:
The welcoming
sitting areas on
Barrie's front
porch feel like
additional "rooms" to
rest and relax in.

Opposite:
A street view of
Barrie's garden-
meets-house

In Barrie's kitchen, garden ivy found its way inside and into the mouth of an antique mounted muskie from the nearby lake.

"There is always a window or door open, so it all feels very connected. The colors in the house are meant to blur the lines between inside and outside."

TO POLLINATE, TO POLLINATE

Barrie's New York garden features puffy clouds of pollinator and cutting plants. In a bed to the right of the house, she planted things like milkweed, echinacea, alliums, and herbs to attract bees, butterflies, and hummingbirds and to have things to clip and bring inside. Her planting plan is tidier than a wild meadow, but the same carefree feeling is there. The voluminous blocks of color are arresting. This idea is something to take into consideration in your own garden, patio, balcony, or wherever a hummingbird or two might linger. After all, there's been much talk of growing "wild lawns" and cutting down on grass to increase the square footage available to pollinating species in order to support surrounding ecosystems. Think of it as the ultimate tribute to beauty and purpose.

Astilbe

Milkweed

Echinacea

Daisies

An Andrew Bush
photograph sets
the fun-loving mood
while the sofa fabric,
"Nympheus," by
GP&J Baker, brings
all the drama of the
garden indoors.

Clockwise from top left:

The pollinator garden bed from the street; D. Porthault floral bedding brings the garden into the guest bedroom; during summer, Barrie entertains friends alfresco most nights so the garden becomes yet another beautiful room to enjoy; tomatoes ripen in the open kitchen window

happen. It makes me a better mother, wife, and designer."

One of the most intoxicating things about the place (of which there are many: the wooden boats on the lake, the no-cars rule, the nightly stimulation of lectures and concerts) is how every single house spills out into the garden around it. There is no inside and outside. Barrie knew straightaway that she wanted to try to grow things she could not cultivate in Charlotte, since the growing zone in New York was entirely different. "In Chautauqua, being able to cut flowers was very important to me, so I consulted with my dear friend and landscape architect Laurie Durden." The result is a garden that billows out and down to the sidewalk. The color palette shifts from red to rose to purple with pops of white and features every romantic bloom possible, from echinacea to lilacs, daisies, anemones, lady's mantle, and Russian sage. Add to that the privacy provided by variegated kousa dogwoods and two varieties of hydrangea, and you begin to understand how lush things are. "Seeing the garden mature has been thrilling," Barrie says. "I love watching each species thrive during different periods of the summer season."

As you might expect, the idea of the garden also features prominently in the decoration of the house, beginning with the porch and kitchen, two natural extensions into the landscape. "There is always a window or door open, so it all feels very connected," she says. She installed the trillium wallpaper by Cole & Son against the original stained wood trim, a nod to the shade of purple flowers that grow abundantly in the garden. "The colors in the house are meant to blur the lines between inside and outside," Barrie says.

But it's the relaxed, open, not-too-precious sense of place that echoes throughout. "There isn't a huge decorating culture in Chautauqua, nor do I want there to be," Barrie says. "That is a part of the reason why I love it so much. I wanted our home to feel very collected. The homes in Chautauqua were built for a very short summer season, so it is all very modest, and I wanted a light hand."

This thought is reflected in the way in which Barrie and her family entertain, too. With ample farms nearby, the kitchen is always filled with local produce (and sweets from Portage Pie). On any given July evening, you're likely to find the Bensons enjoying supper on the porch or having their neighbors over to enjoy homemade pizza straight out the wood-fired oven in the garden. And since Chautauqua has hosted the same sort of festivities for over a century, Barrie hopes the magical traditions continue. "I really fell in love with the intergenerational aspect of Chautauqua, too," Barrie says. "The homes are filled with grandparents and parents and children. It's just a very special place to make memories." ■

Lia's watercolor work covers an array of botanical subjects and brings humor and lightness to a traditional genre.

Watercolors

by Lia Burke Libaire of Lia Burke Libaire Art & Design,
Charleston, South Carolina

The geraniums are what started it for me. But really all of it: the sprigs of citrus, the pitcher plants, the technicolor mushrooms. This ethereal cutting garden and potager plot I'm speaking of grows in the imagination of the Charleston, South Carolina, watercolor artist Lia Burke Libaire. "Plants or flowers in a room bring it alive, literally and aesthetically," Lia says. "And of course, [botanical] art-work is not the same as an actual living thing, but I certainly think it can invoke many of the same feelings." I agree, and I also believe it's human nature to crave exposure to the great outdoors; I think it's critical for our emotional and phys-ical health. Which is exactly why Lia's watercolors create a window into a gar-den that anyone can enjoy indoors, at any time, even if it's pouring down rain outside.

When I first met Lia, she was on the early side of her creative ascent, and in the time since, her breezy and often tongue-in-cheek approach to a classic subject has exploded in popularity. I appreciated not only the airiness of her things (they seem to float in a wash of color or plain white and feel calming) but also her obvious sense of humor and fun and especially the thoughtful way she frames her pieces to sell them. "Botanicals are beautiful and timeless, but no one would claim that it's an original idea to paint them," she says. "I think bringing a sense of wit helps to differentiate my work from some other very talented artists out there; it's infused with a part of my personality." Fast-forward just a few short years and Lia now produces custom collections for retail elites like Kate Rheinstein Brodsky of KRB in New York and Kate Holt of the ARK Elements in Los Angeles.

Lia often produces these new collec-tions in rushes of creativity followed by lulls of rest preparing for the next

Paper that Lia uses to dab and dry her brushes while working is a work of art in and of itself.

"[BOTANICAL] ARTWORK IS NOT THE SAME AS AN ACTUAL LIVING THING, BUT I CERTAINLY THINK IT CAN INVOKE MANY OF THE SAME FEELINGS."

moment an idea descends. "When I am feeling especially inspired and like I need to get a particular idea out of my brain, everything else can suffer because I'm so distracted by it," she says. "In those moments, I know it's time to put pen to paper." A calligraphy pen, to be specific. Once the ink dries, then Lia applies the watercolors to every piece at the same time. "I usually do this so that the hand looks consistent between all the pieces in a series," she says. "I can't move forward with one until all are in the same phase." Then come the very special frames and mats, many of which Lia also paints. "I am very aware that most of my artwork plays a role in creating a bigger picture, so it's always part of my process."

Lia's background in interiors and understanding how designers think also led her into a wallpaper collaboration with her close friend, the Los Angeles interior designer Georgia Tapert Howe (who we visited in chapter 3; see page 155). "I had been told that my artwork would lend itself well to wallpaper, and the idea sounded intriguing, but it didn't feel like something I could realistically tackle. My daughter was a small baby at the time, and I was just diving into being a full-time artist. Then, Georgia asked about collaborating on some wallpaper designs," Lia remembers. "Slowly Brier & Byrd was born, named for both of our daughters. It was certainly not a quick beginning; it took a long time to create many of the patterns and to get them to where we wanted them to be. Then, of course, COVID-19 happened, which slowed things further, but in the end, it was worth the wait." So far, Artichoke Vine, which is on full display at Hollywood at Home in Los Angeles, is a clear winner, but Lia says she's constantly surprised at what resonates with customers. "We hope that our patterns are timeless and classic, but updated and cleaner than most of the traditional botanical textiles that are out there."

These days, with two littles in tow, a blossoming career, and a full house renovation underway, Lia welcomes a little amble in the prolific garden beyond her kitchen door. "There are many mature fruit trees, lots of kumquats, loquats, persimmons, lemons, blood oranges, and fig—all of which were in pretty great shape when we moved in," she says. "Citrus is my first love, but they will all get their turn as my subjects." ■

Opposite: Lia's airy take on botanicals often features calligraphy ink sketches paired with colorful watercolor washes.

Study COBALT

BRAQUENIÉ

BRIER & BYRD

BRIER & BYRD

Happy bday to my darling
What would I do withou[t]
[m]iss you every single minut[e]
[of ever]y single day and I dream
[that] we can eat together aga[in]
[I] love you more than all [the]
McDonald's and Melfi's
Bachelor episodes put tog[ether]

Love, Taylor (+ Foxy +[ )]

1981NYC.COM

HAPPY

Opposite: Lia's
mood board of
many colors

This page: Lia in
her studio

Epilogue
SOUL

A watercolor portrait of the house on Grove Street, by Charleston artist Barbara Beach

A detail of my beloved painting by Charleston artist Ann Keane. It hung in the living room on Grove Street and now graces the kitchen of my new house.

ONE ART

by Elizabeth Bishop

The art of losing isn't hard to master;
so many things seem filled with the intent
to be lost that their loss is no disaster.

Lose something every day. Accept the fluster
of lost door keys, the hour badly spent.
The art of losing isn't hard to master.

Then practice losing farther, losing faster:
places, and names, and where it was you meant
to travel. None of these will bring disaster.

I lost my mother's watch. And look! my last, or
next-to-last, of three houses went.
The art of losing isn't hard to master.

I lost two cities, lovely ones. And, vaster,
some realms I owned, two rivers, a continent.
I missed them, but it wasn't a disaster.

—Even losing you (the joking voice, a gesture
I love) I shan't have lied. It's evident
the art of losing's not too hard to master
though it may look like (*Write* it!) like disaster.

I have the same dream at least once a month. I'm in the kitchen of the farmhouse our family no longer owns. It's very early. There is bacon cooking in a cast-iron skillet on the old Viking stove my dad salvaged and repaired part by part. There is frost on the windows. Or I'm outside, running up the hill from the lake to the house, and it's July, and as the tall grass parts, bugs of every stripe take flight. I am eight. It feels safe.

And then it's not. I see a stranger's car parked outside, and the house morphs into something I don't know, and I remember it's not ours anymore, and I'm trespassing. Then I wake up.

I have a similar dream about Grove Street. It's because I lost her. Sacrificed her to the chaos of life, in this case a heartbreaking and very necessary divorce. This doesn't mean that love didn't live there in its complicated way. Quite the opposite, especially in the years after becoming a mother. Grove Street held friends and family and parties and dinners and quiet afternoons.

She witnessed.

Houses do that. She is the fifth I've loved deeply and no longer call mine.

Everyone loses a house in life at one time or another, which really is why homes are more than shelter. They are characters, souls, friends.

I haven't been back to my house in Birmingham in nearly twenty years. I want to remember her as she was, I guess. Or

the farm. Same thing there. I find it too painful to step backward. I know change would greet me like a slap.

In contrast, I *did* want to stop by my childhood home a few months ago with my son. I'm not sure why, but I felt as if she might still be well cared for. She was not. The brick walls my dad built with his hands to create a secret garden for us as children looked as if they'd been bombed out, reduced to tumbles of rubble in the overgrown green grass. The roof and verandas drooped with age.

My first reactions were anger and sadness. I rolled down the car window and stared at her for a long time, all the while telling my little boy what she used to look like and where I used to play and run with his aunt and uncle. And then it occurred to me that loving a house is the ultimate test of living in the present. There is no real control over what does and does not become of them in the "after." The only way to truly honor a deep and abiding love for homes is to bring a bit of their souls to the next and the next and the next.

I drove away hopeful.

That all happened during an excruciating in-between time when I was searching for a new house at arguably the worst time in many decades to purchase real estate. For many months, I shared a tiny temporary apartment with my little boy, with all of our things in storage. At first, I thought I wouldn't survive being wrenched from all that had been famil-

Clockwise from bottom: The story in Southern Living *about the cottage I fixed up; the Georgian house I grew up in; me, age five, in the garden my parents made so enchanting*

iar, and I worried about him as well. But then I started taping photos of beautiful rooms to the walls and we started dreaming together. We talked about what we liked in the pictures, what we loved about our old house, and what we thought our next house might look like and where we might land. Pretty soon, the whole apartment was a mood board of sorts. Imagining the comforts of what might one day be ours gave us a place to come home to in our mind.

And at long last I found a quiet cottage for us on a barrier island outside of Charleston to start over in. I'm already bringing the spirit of all my other places, and many of the ideas we tethered our-

selves to while living in limbo, to live with us here. The whole thing is a completely divergent experience for me—a house built just twenty years ago to look like something far older than her years. Unlike a lot of newer construction, this home already has many of the details that give the illusion of age and character, and I plan to add even more.

So far, I've painted the floors white, unpacked nearly all the boxes, and started kitchen and bath renovations. There is much, much more to go. Only time will tell what fun is in store for this gem, the sixth in a long legacy of loved houses. ∎

My little boy checking out the walls I'm painting in our new house

"The only way
to truly honor
a deep and abiding
love for homes is
to bring a bit of their
souls to the next
and the next and
the next."

RESOURCES
&
CREDITS

RESOURCES

Paint at the ready at my new house

1
MEANING
*Places for
Special Finds*

Mail-Order Framing

Framebridge
framebridge.com

Simply Framed
simplyframed.com

All Things
Vintage, Antique,
Artisanal,
and Small-Batch

214 Modern Vintage
214modernvintage.com

Chairish
chairish.com

Field + Supply
fieldandsupply.com

Penland School of Craft
penland.org

Further Reading

*Collected: Living with the
Things You Love*, by Fritz Karch
and Rebecca Robertson

2
COMFORT
Sensory Items

Linens and Soft Goods

Annie Selke
annieselke.com

Biscuit
biscuit-home.com

Coco & Wolf
cocoandwolf.com

Heather Taylor Home
heathertaylorhome.com

Loretta Caponi
lorettacaponi.it

Overland
overland.com

Peacock Alley
peacockalley.com

Serena & Lily
serenaandlily.com

Tabletop

The ARK Elements
thearkelements.com

Dear Keaton
dearkeaton.com

etúHOME
etuhome.com

Food52
food52.com

Ginny Sims
ginnysimsceramics.com

Madame de la Maison
madamedelamaison.com

Maison Flâneur
maisonflaneur.com

Massey Gordon
massey-gordon.myshopify.com

Morgan Levine Ceramics
morganlevineceramics.com

Odd McClean
oddmclean.com

Self-Care

HONNA
honnalondon.com

Klei
kleibeauty.com

Loop
loopcanvas.com

One Love Organics
oneloveorganics.com

Sangre de Fruta
sangredefruta.com

Upholstery

Coley Home
coleyhome.com

Rifle Paper Co. x Cloth & Company
riflepaperco.com

Pantry

La Colombe Coffee Roasters
lacolombe.com

Mariage Frères
mariagefreres.com

Further Reading

*Where Cooking Begins:
Uncomplicated Recipes to
Make You a Great Cook,*
by Carla Lalli Music

3
AUTHENTICITY
*Things with
Staying Power*

Window Treatments

Wovn Home
wovnhome.com

Tile

New Ravenna
newravenna.com

Plumbing, Lighting, and Hardware

Circa Lighting
circalighting.com

Kohler
kohler.com

Rejuvenation
rejuvenation.com

Schoolhouse
schoolhouse.com

Water Monopoly
thewatermonopoly.com

Accessories

Flying Geese
flyinggeese.co

Replacements, Ltd.
replacements.com

Paint

Backdrop
backdrophome.com

Farrow & Ball
farrow-ball.com

Little Greene
littlegreene.com

Further Reading

*Creating a New Old
House: Yesterday's
Character for Today's Home,*
by Russell Versaci

4
FLAIR
Decorative Accents

Fabrics, Fine Art Papers, and Wallpapers

Adelphi Paper Hangings
adelphipaperhangings.com

Anna Spiro Textiles
annaspirotextiles.com.au

Brier & Byrd
brierandbyrd.com

The Design Social Studio
thedesignsocialstudio.com

Fine Art Store
www.fineartstore.com

Fritz Porter
fritzporter.com

Hollywood at Home
hollywoodathome.com

House of Hackney
houseofhackney.com

James Showroom
jamesshowroom.com

Kiki Slaughter
kikislaughter.com

The Lot
thelotshowroom.com

Mulberry Paper
mulberrypaperandmore.com

Schumacher
schumacher.com

Studio Four NYC
studiofournyc.com

Supply Showroom
supplyshowroom.com

Talas Online
talasonline.com

Temple
templestudio.us

Inspiring Shops

Amanda Lindroth
amandalindroth.com

Archive New York
archivenewyork.com

Beata Heuman
beataheuman.com

Cutter Brooks
cutterbrooks.com

Furbish
furbishstudio.com

Get the Gusto
getthegusto.com

Houses & Parties
housesandparties.com

KRB
krbnyc.com

Nickey Kehoe
nickeykehoe.com

Pentreath & Hall
pentreath-hall.com

Sharland England by Louise Roe
sharland-england.com

Utilitario Mexicano
utilitariomexicano.com

Wicklewood
wicklewood.com

Further Reading

The Authentics: A Lush Dive into the Substance of Style, by Melanie Acevedo and Dara Caponigro

---

5
NATURE
Garden Goods

Furniture and Accessories

The Floral Society
thefloralsociety.com

Gardenheir
gardenheir.com

Hay
us.hay.com

Terrain
shopterrain.com

Botanical Art

The Green Vase
thegreenvase.com

Lia Burke Libaire
liaburkelibaire.com

Marian McEvoy
krbnyc.com

Urban Garden
urbangardenprints.com

Plants and Flowers

Antique Rose Emporium
antiqueroseemporium.com

Floret
floretflowers.com

Further Reading

The Well-Gardened Mind: The Restorative Power of Nature, by Sue Stuart-Smith

EPILOGUE
SOUL
On Memorializing a House

Architectural Watercolors

Barbara Beach
Instagram: @bbeachbb

Further Reading

A Family Place: A Man Returns to the Center of His Life, by Charles Gaines

CREDITS

Page 20
"Petite Fruit" linen, by Wayne Pate + Studio Four NYC

studiofournyc.com

Page 68
"Improvisation 1," by Ottoline

ottoline.co.uk

Page 25
"#012 Pierrette," by Les Indiennes

studiofournyc.com

Page 74
"Beatrice," by Alice Sergeant

alicesergeant.com

Page 28
"Mizu" linen, by Studio Four NYC

studiofournyc.com

Page 88
"Rainbow Rose," by House of Hackney

houseofhackney.com

Page 34
"Petite Zoebel" linen, by Wayne Pate + Studio Four NYC

studiofournyc.com

Page 102
"Eden," from The Cloth Shop

theclothshop.net

Pages 44–45
"David" linen, by CW Stockwell x Voutsa Martinique© Celebration!

voutsa.com

Page 122
"Ziggy in Cloudcroft," by Kufri

kufrilifefabrics.com

Page 170
**"Marbleized Velvet," by
Beata Heuman**

beataheuman.com

Page 174
**"Lattice" wrapping paper,
from Pentreath & Hall**

pentreath-hall.com

Page 177
**"Tortoise" wrapping paper,
by Caspari**

casparionline.com

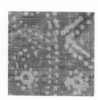

Page 210
**"Zig Zag," by Carolina
Irving Textiles**

carolinairvingtextiles.com

ACKNOWLEDGMENTS

The year that this book came to be was one of the most difficult of my life, and this project would have fizzled away into the ether of a thousand other worries had it not been for two people: Jan Baumer and Charlotte Zacharkiw. Jan is my agent, but also a friend from my long-ago youth (we worked together as maids at a dude ranch in Wyoming—true story), who believed I had something unique to bring to the world of interior design books. I am still dumbfounded that any of this is happening. Jan is not. And for that I have endless buckets of gratitude.

Charlotte is responsible for the beautiful photographs in this book. She is also one of my closest friends. She, too, believed I could pull off a miracle. We traveled all over the world, side by side, for nearly a year, fitting in photo shoots in between raising children (my one, her three) and keeping our day jobs. There was big, tear-jerking laughter and collaboration at every turn, and Charlotte's presence and contributions taught me what a healthy, supportive relationship looks like—which is the gift of a lifetime.

As my adventures with Charlotte unfolded, my frequent collaborator and general contractor for the last eighteen years, John Harrelson, kept the progress at my new house going—even when I was a continent away. John also lifted my spirits on hard days with quick jokes and unending patience for both my grief and my ideas for the future. I would be lost without his kindness.

With each visit, I also felt more and more appreciation for the women featured in the book for letting us invade their lives. It's an intimate thing to photograph a home, and I'm forever thankful for getting to know each woman and experience each space.

Finally, the book-building process is fascinating, and the women I've come to know during it all at Abrams created an environment of stewardship, healing, and support. So much so that I think I cried happy tears at the first art meeting. From day one, I could feel my new wings sprouting, but they would never have grown to fruition without all of these talented cheerleaders. ■

Editor: Laura Dozier
Designer: Alaina Sullivan
Design Manager: Danny Maloney
Managing Editor: Annalea Manalili
Production Manager: Alison Gervais

Library of Congress Control Number: 2023941977

ISBN: 978-1-4197-6808-8
eISBN: 979-8-88707-025-4

Text copyright © 2024 Haskell Harris
Photographs copyright © 2024 Charlotte Zacharkiwe, except:
Pages 9–12 by Martina Gemmola
Illustrations copyright © 2024 Lia Burke Libaire

Page 7: From *The Measure of a Man*, by Sidney Poitier. Copyright © 2000 by
Sidney Poitier. Used by permission of HarperCollins Publishers.
Page 257: "One Art," from *The Complete Poems 1927–1979*, by Elizabeth
Bishop. Copyright © 2011 by The Alice H. Methfessel Trust. Publisher's Note
and compilation copyright © 2011 by Farrar, Straus and Giroux. Reprinted by
permission of Farrar, Straus and Giroux. All Rights Reserved.

Cover © 2024 Abrams

Published in 2024 by Abrams, an imprint of ABRAMS. All rights reserved.
No portion of this book may be reproduced, stored in a retrieval system, or
transmitted in any form or by any means, mechanical, electronic, photocopying,
recording, or otherwise, without written permission from the publisher.

Printed and bound in China
10 9 8 7 6 5 4 3 2 1

Abrams books are available at special discounts when purchased in
quantity for premiums and promotions as well as fundraising or educational use.
Special editions can also be created to specification.
For details, contact specialsales@abramsbooks.com or the address below.

Abrams® is a registered trademark of Harry N. Abrams, Inc.

ABRAMS The Art of Books
195 Broadway, New York, NY 10007
abramsbooks.com